ONE
TIN
BAKES

Edd Kimber

ONE
TIN
BAKES

Edd Kimber
@THEBOYWHOBAKES

PHOTOGRAPHY BY EDD KIMBER

KYLE BOOKS

An Hachette UK Company
www.hachette.co.uk

First published in Great Britain in 2020 by
Kyle Books, an imprint of Kyle Cathie Ltd
Carmelite House
50 Victoria Embankment
London EC4Y 0DZ
www.kylebooks.co.uk

ISBN: 978 0 85783 859 9

Distributed in the US by Hachette Book Group, 1290 Avenue of the Americas,
4th and 5th Floors, New York, NY 10104

Distributed in Canada by Canadian Manda Group, 664 Annette St., Toronto,
Ontario, Canada M6S 2C8

Editorial Director: Judith Hannam
Publisher: Joanna Copestick
Editor: Isabel Gonzalez-Prendergast
Design: Evi O Studio | Evi O., Nicole Ho & Kait Polkinghorne
Photography & Food Styling: Edd Kimber*
Production: Gemma John & Nic Jones

*image on page 175 © Simon Kimber

A Cataloguing in Publication record for this title is available
from the British Library

Printed and bound in China

10 9 8 7 6 5

INTRO

This is a book for home bakers, those who bake after a long day's work and those who love to bake but don't have a magical cupboard full of every baking vessel known to man.

I love baking. I spend each and every day in the kitchen playing around with butter, sugar, eggs and flour, and I sometimes joke that it's the only thing I am actually any good at. I've spent the last ten years encouraging people to embrace the flour-covered apron, the freezer full of cookie dough and the random splatter of cake batter that inexplicably appears on the ceiling. In those ten years I've tried to write recipes that are designed for the home baker and I've pitched recipes with varying degrees of complexity to write books that are approachable and useable, but also encourage you to try something more involved when you have the confidence. The recipes suit many different situations, from a simple dessert for the family at the weekend to recipes perfect for a party.

In my previous book *Patisserie Made Simple*, I also tried to reduce the amount of equipment needed to make beautiful and delicious bakes. *One Tin Bakes* is the ultimate culmination of those ideas, reducing the required bakeware to just one simple tin.

Each and every recipe in this book is baked in just one tin, a 23 x 33cm (9 x 13in) cake tin (commonly used for brownies). For this book you won't end up with bakeware falling out of every cupboard and hidden under your bed, it is just one tin bakes.

The obvious question is why this tin, why not a sheet pan, a set of round cake tins or even a loaf pan? I believe this tin is the most flexible, the most multipurpose, the most useful tin there is. It is a mainstay of any baker's arsenal and in my book (literally this book, you're reading it right now) it should be the hero. In it, you can make cookies, cakes, desserts, brownies, pies and tarts. In fact, if you can bake it, you can probably bake it in one of these tins. I also chose the tin because it's already popular, it can do it all and if you bake there is a good chance you already own one, and if you don't you'll find them in every cookware shop going.

THE TIN

When it comes to choosing the right tin there are a few things to bear in mind. With these recipes, depth is crucial. You will need a version of the tin that is at least 5cm (2in) deep. This will ensure everything bakes without any issues. While testing these recipes I tried many brands and variations and one thing became clear: every manufacturer measures 23 x 33cm (9 x 13in) a little differently – some are a little wider, some a little shorter, they all vary. To account for these variations, use a tin that is at least 5cm (2in) deep and all the recipes will fit without any issues.

With this style of tin you also have a choice between metal, glass and ceramic, plus a variety of different finishes. For the mix of recipe styles in this book I'm not a fan of glass or ceramic, for me metal suits a broader spectrum of recipes and is the obvious choice. The style I would recommend is an aluminium tin. This is a classic bakeware choice and it will happily stand the test of time. It tends to bake and brown evenly and is lightweight. My favourite comes from Nordicware, one of the oldest and best bakeware manufacturers in the world. The one style I avoid and would recommend you do too is a non-stick tin with a dark/black coating. These absorb and distribute heat more quickly, leading to recipes browning too much and possibly burning. They are also more prone to damage. If this is the tin you already own, then bake at a slightly reduced temperature and check for doneness a few minutes earlier than the recipe calls for.

HOW TO LINE THE TIN

There are four methods used to prepare the tin:

1. Simply greasing the tin without a parchment lining – used for recipes served from the tin.

2. Just lining the base with parchment – used for recipes portioned inside the tin as the parchment helps prevent the base from sticking.

3. Using a strip of parchment with the excess going up the long sides of the tin, held in place with metal clips – used when a bake needs to be lifted from the tin after baking, with the parchment acting like a sling.

4. Lining the whole tin with one single sheet of parchment – used when the recipe has a tendency to stick to the sides, making it harder to remove.

CAKES

MILK CHOCOLATE CARAMEL SHEET CAKE

SERVES 12–15

This recipe is the reason this book exists, my OG one tin cake that has fed countless crowds as I developed the recipe. One early version came with me to the local pub, and once my friends had devoured most of it, we handed out the rest to strangers – a cake is still the best way I know to make friends. The ganache is made with a bittersweet salted caramel and topped with peanuts and cacao nibs. If there is one cake I want you to try, it's this one.

FOR THE MILK CHOCOLATE SALTED CARAMEL GANACHE

200g (7oz) milk chocolate, finely chopped

400ml (14fl oz/1⅔ cups) double (heavy) cream

200g (7oz/1 cup) caster (superfine) sugar

50g (1¾oz/3½ tablespoons) unsalted butter

1 teaspoon flaked sea salt

1 teaspoon vanilla extract

FOR THE CHOCOLATE SHEET CAKE

250g (9oz/2 cups) plain (all-purpose) flour

75g (2¾oz/¾ cup + 2 tablespoons) cocoa powder

1 teaspoon baking powder

2 teaspoons bicarbonate of soda

½ teaspoon fine sea salt

300g (10½oz/1⅓ cups + 1 teaspoon) light brown sugar

2 large eggs

100ml (3½fl oz/⅓ cup + 4 teaspoons) neutral-tasting oil, plus extra for greasing

225ml (8fl oz/1 cup – 1 tablespoon) sour cream

225ml (8fl oz/1 cup – 1 tablespoon) hot brewed coffee

TO DECORATE

salted peanuts

cacao nibs

First, make the ganache as it needs to chill before use. Place the chocolate in a large, heatproof bowl. Pour the cream into a small saucepan, bring to a simmer, then remove from the heat. Heat the sugar in a medium-sized saucepan over a medium heat until melted and the colour of an old copper coin. Add the butter, salt and half the warm cream. Once the bubbling has subsided, you should have a smooth caramel. If not, reduce the heat and stir until smooth. Pour in the remaining cream and the vanilla and stir to combine.

While still hot, pour the caramel over the chocolate and leave for a couple of minutes, then stir until a smooth ganache. Cover and refrigerate for a couple of hours or until the texture of buttercream, soft and scoopable. If you leave it too long it will thicken and whipping the ganache will become tough.

Preheat the oven to 180°C (350°F), Gas Mark 4. Lightly grease the baking tin and line with a piece of parchment paper that overhangs the two long sides of the tin, securing in place with metal clips.

Sift the flour, cocoa powder, baking powder, bicarbonate of soda, salt and sugar into a large bowl and whisk to combine. Make a well in the middle, pour in all the remaining ingredients and whisk everything together just until smooth. Pour the batter into the prepared tin and spread evenly.

Bake for 25–30 minutes or until the cake springs back to a light touch and is starting to pull away from the tin's sides.

Because the cake is on the large side, it is a little harder to manoeuvre, so cool in the tin for 20–30 minutes, before using the overhanging parchment paper to lift it to a wire rack to cool completely.

Use an electric mixer to whisk the ganache for a few minutes until smooth and shiny (over-whisking can make it grainy, so err on the side of caution). Spread over the cake, then sprinkle liberally with peanuts and cacao nibs. Cut into portions and serve.

Store in a sealed container for 4–5 days.

CAKES

'COFFEE' COFFEE CAKE

SERVES 12–15

Although a coffee cake is one that is served with coffee rather than one actually made with it, I still feel a little short-changed when coffee cake is missing its main identifying ingredient. So to correct decades of baking injustice, I've snuck espresso powder into this otherwise classic coffee cake. The sour cream gives the cake a little tang and results in a wonderfully textured cake that stays moist for days.

FOR THE BROWN BUTTER STREUSEL

125g (4½oz/1 stick + 1 tablespoon) unsalted butter, plus extra for greasing

160g (5¾oz/1¼ cups) plain (all-purpose) flour

115g (4oz/½ cup + 1 heaped tablespoon) caster (superfine) sugar

½ teaspoon fine sea salt

FOR THE ESPRESSO SWIRL

100g (3½oz/⅓ cup + 2 tablespoons) light brown sugar

3 teaspoons instant espresso powder

2 teaspoons ground cinnamon

FOR THE SOUR CREAM CAKE

175g (6oz/1½ sticks + 1 teaspoon) unsalted butter, at room temperature

300g (10½oz/1½ cups) caster (superfine) sugar

315g (11oz/2½ cups) plain (all-purpose) flour

1 tablespoon baking powder

1 teaspoon fine sea salt

1 teaspoon vanilla extract

3 large eggs

180ml (6¼fl oz/¾ cup) sour cream

Preheat the oven to 180°C (350°F), Gas Mark 4. Lightly grease the baking tin and line with a piece of parchment paper that overhangs the two long sides of the tin and secure in place with metal clips.

Start by making the streusel as it needs to chill a little before baking. Mix the flour, sugar and salt together in a bowl. Melt the butter in a small saucepan over a medium heat, stirring frequently. The butter will melt, sizzle and splatter and then start to foam. As it foams, little golden brown flecks will start to appear. Before these flecks burn, remove the pan from the heat and pour the butter over the dry ingredients, using a fork to stir until it all clumps together. You're looking for a mix of fine crumbs and big chunks. Pop the bowl into the freezer.

Next, make the espresso swirl. Mix together the sugar, espresso powder and cinnamon in a small bowl and set aside.

For the cake, place the butter and sugar into the bowl of an electric stand mixer fitted with the paddle attachment and mix on medium speed for 5 minutes, or until light and fluffy. Meanwhile, mix together the flour, baking powder and salt in a separate bowl. Add the vanilla to the butter mixture and mix briefly to combine. Add the eggs, one at a time, beating until fully combined before adding another. Add the flour mixture in three batches, alternating with the sour cream, starting and finishing with the flour.

Spoon two-thirds of the cake batter into the prepared tin, spreading into an even layer. Sprinkle over the espresso swirl then dot small spoonfuls of the remaining batter all over the top, covering as much of the swirl mixture as possible before gently spreading so that all of the swirl mixture is covered. Sprinkle over the streusel in an even layer.

Bake for 45–50 minutes or until a skewer inserted into the middle of the cake comes out clean. Leave to cool in the tin for about 15–20 minutes, before using the parchment paper to gently lift it out on to a wire rack to cool completely. Once cool, cut into portions and serve.

Store in a sealed container for 2–3 days.

ALMOND AND MIXED BERRY DUMP CAKE

SERVES 8–10

Can we talk about the name of this cake? I understand that it's not the prettiest or most enticing name, but this recipe is inspired by a style of recipe referred to as 'dump cakes' – a cake where a fruit filling is topped with a boxed cake mix and a few pieces of butter, then baked. The result is not my favourite, a little dry and powdery, more cobbler than cake. I do, however, like the idea of expediency and spontaneity, so this recipe is a simple cake mix you can keep in your cupboard, and with the addition of a couple of other basic ingredients, stirred together in the tin, you can whip up a simple snack cake in minutes.

FOR THE ALMOND CAKE MIX

200g (7oz/2 cups) ground almonds

200g (7oz/1⅔ cups) icing (powdered) sugar

50g (1¾oz/⅓ cup + 1 tablespoon) plain (all-purpose) flour

30g (1oz/2 tablespoons) egg white powder

½ teaspoon baking powder

½ teaspoon fine sea salt

FOR THE BAKE AND TOPPINGS

200g (7oz/1¾ sticks) unsalted butter, melted, plus extra for greasing

160ml (5½fl oz/⅔ cup) whole milk

1 teaspoon vanilla extract

300g (10½oz) mixed fresh or frozen berries

3 tablespoons chopped nuts (I prefer pistachios)

To make the cake mix, pop all the ingredients into a large bowl and whisk together to combine. Scoop the mix into a large, airtight jar and store until needed.

When you want to make the cake, preheat the oven to 180°C (350°F), Gas Mark 4. Lightly grease the baking tin and line the base with a piece of parchment paper.

Tip the cake mix into the prepared baking tin, then pour in the melted butter, milk and vanilla and mix together briefly using a spatula until fairly well combined. Spread into an even layer and sprinkle over the berries and nuts.

Bake for about 30 minutes or until the edges of the cake are starting to brown and the centre is set.

Leave the cake to cool completely in the tin, before cutting into pieces to serve.

This cake is best enjoyed on the day it's made.

PASSION FRUIT AND LIME TRES LECHES CAKE

SERVES 10

Tres leches (three milk), is a classic cake from South America. The sponge, or sometimes butter cake, is soaked in a mix of three milks, usually sweetened condensed milk, evaporated milk and whole milk or cream. The soaked sponge, topped with whipped cream, is pure comfort, and reminds me a little of trifle in texture. The original is close to perfect, but I wanted to make something with a few favourite flavours – passion fruit, lime and coconut plus, if you're in the mood, a splash or two of rum.

unsalted butter or neutral-tasting oil, for greasing

FOR THE SPONGE CAKE

1 batch of sponge cake mixture (see page 34)

finely grated zest of 2 limes

FOR THE SOAK

120ml (4fl oz/½ cup) whole milk

finely grated zest of 2 limes

397g (14oz) can condensed milk

240ml (8½fl oz/1 cup) light coconut milk

60ml (2¼fl oz/¼ cup) dark rum (optional)

160ml (5½fl oz/⅔ cup) passion fruit purée

FOR THE TOPPING

600ml (20fl oz/2½ cups) double (heavy) cream

finely grated zest of 2 limes

1 tablespoon caster (superfine) sugar

pulp from 3 passion fruit

30g (1oz/⅓ cup) toasted coconut flakes

Preheat the oven to 180°C (350°F), Gas Mark 4. Lightly grease the baking tin, then line with a large piece of parchment paper so that the excess goes up the sides.

Prepare the sponge cake according to the instructions on page 34, adding the lime zest to the warmed butter and milk mixture, allowing it to infuse as the butter cools.

Pour the cake batter into the prepared baking tin and gently level out. Bake for 25–30 minutes or until the cake is golden brown and springs back to a gentle touch. Set aside to cool in the tin for 30 minutes while you make the soak.

Pour the milk into a small saucepan and warm slightly (don't bring it to a simmer), then remove from the heat, add the lime zest and set aside to cool for 30 minutes. Whisk in the condensed milk, coconut milk and rum (if using).

Use a skewer to poke holes all over the top of the cake and then pour over the passion fruit purée. Once this has sat for a couple of minutes, slowly pour over the milk and lime mixture, then set aside until the milk has been fully absorbed. You don't mix the passion fruit purée into the milk mixture because it can thicken the milk, meaning it won't absorb into the cake in the same way. Cover the cake and refrigerate for at least 4 hours.

For the topping, whip the cream, zest of 1 lime and the sugar together in a bowl until just holding soft peaks. Spread the cream over the chilled cake and then top with the passion fruit pulp, flaked coconut and remaining lime zest. Cut into portions and serve.

Store, covered, in the refrigerator for about 4 days.

ONE BOWL VANILLA SHEET CAKE

SERVES 12

Just like my chocolate sheet cake, my perfect vanilla cake is a one-bowl affair made with buttermilk for a little tang and a wonderful moist texture. A great vanilla cake deserves a very special buttercream, so for this recipe, I have turned to a super smooth and silky Swiss meringue version. You can make this cake with ridiculously little effort and then while it bakes, you can quickly knock up the buttercream. As vanilla is the dominant flavour, this is a recipe for which I would splurge and use a vanilla pod for the buttercream.

FOR THE VANILLA SHEET CAKE

400g (14oz/3¼ cups) plain (all-purpose) flour

1¼ teaspoons baking powder

2½ teaspoons bicarbonate of soda

1 teaspoon salt

400g (14oz/2 cups) caster (superfine) sugar

3 large eggs

135ml (4½fl oz/½ cup + 1 tablespoon) neutral-tasting oil (I prefer canola)

285ml (9½fl oz/1 cup + 3 tablespoons) buttermilk

1 tablespoon vanilla extract

240ml (8½fl oz/1 cup) boiling water

FOR THE SWISS MERINGUE BUTTERCREAM

240g (8¾oz/2 sticks + 1 tablespoon) unsalted butter, diced and at room temperature, plus extra for greasing

2 large egg whites

⅛ teaspoon cream of tartar

pinch of salt

150g (5½oz/¾ cup) caster (superfine) sugar

seeds scraped from 1 vanilla pod

sprinkles, to decorate (optional)

Preheat the oven to 180°C (350°F), Gas Mark 4. Lightly grease the baking tin and line with a piece of parchment paper that overhangs the two long sides.

For the cake, add the flour, baking powder, bicarbonate of soda, salt and sugar to a large bowl and whisk to combine. Make a well in the middle, add in the eggs, oil, buttermilk and vanilla, then whisk until the batter is smooth and combined. Pour in the boiling water and whisk briefly to mix. The batter will be thin, but don't worry, that's what we want.

Pour the batter into the prepared tin, then bake for 35–40 minutes or until a skewer inserted into the middle comes out clean.

Leave the cake to cool in the tin for 20 minutes, before using the overhanging parchment paper to lift it on to a wire rack to cool completely.

To make the buttercream, place the egg whites, cream of tartar, salt, sugar and vanilla into a large heatproof bowl and place over a pan of simmering water (ensuring the bottom of the bowl doesn't touch the water underneath), stirring regularly until the sugar has dissolved and the mixture is hot to the touch.

Remove from the heat and using an electric mixer whisk for 7–10 minutes until room temperature. Then slowly add the butter, a piece or two at a time. Mix until the mixture forms a buttercream-like texture and is silky smooth.

Spread the buttercream over the cooled cake and top with sprinkles (if using). Cut into portions and serve.

Store, covered, for 3 days.

NOTE Don't discard the used vanilla pod, there is a ton of flavour left inside. You can use it to roast fruits, to make vanilla sugar or even to infuse a simple syrup.

COCONUT SHEET CAKE

SERVES 12–15

Coconut cake is pure comfort. I didn't grow up with it, it holds no nostalgic memories for me so I can't quite pinpoint why this is. Maybe it's the simplicity, the fact that there's nothing but cake and frosting, nothing complicated, nothing fancy. I have squeezed as much coconut as I can into this recipe, so the cake is made with coconut oil and butter and includes desiccated coconut and a little coconut extract. The frosting is a classic cream cheese one covered in a heavy snowfall of coconut; it's coconut squared.

FOR THE COCONUT SHEET CAKE

115g (4oz/½ cup) unsalted butter, at room temperature, plus extra for greasing

115g (4oz/½ cup) virgin coconut oil

350g (12oz/1¾ cups) caster (superfine) sugar

420g (15oz/3⅓ cups) plain (all-purpose) flour

4 teaspoons baking powder

1 teaspoon fine sea salt

2 teaspoons vanilla extract

2 teaspoons coconut extract

5 large egg whites

350ml (12fl oz/1⅓ cups + 2 tablespoons) coconut milk

85g (3oz/1 cup) desiccated coconut

FOR THE CREAM CHEESE FROSTING

75g (2¾oz/⅔ stick) unsalted butter, at room temperature

125g (4½oz/½ cup + 1 tablespoon) full-fat cream cheese, at room temperature

400g (14oz/3⅓ cups) icing sugar

¼ teaspoon fine sea salt

2 teaspoons vanilla extract

60g (2¼oz/⅔ cup) desiccated coconut, to decorate

Preheat the oven to 180°C (350°F), Gas Mark 4. Lightly grease the baking tin and line with a strip of parchment paper that overhangs the two long sides, securing in place with metal clips.

For the cake, place the butter, coconut oil and caster sugar into a large bowl and using an electric mixer beat together on medium speed for 7–8 minutes, or until light and fluffy.

Meanwhile, mix together the flour, baking powder and salt in a separate bowl. Add the vanilla and coconut extracts to the butter mixture and mix briefly to combine, then add the egg whites, one at a time, mixing until fully combined before adding another. Add the flour mixture in three additions alternating with the coconut milk, starting and finishing with the flour. Fold in the desiccated coconut.

Scrape the cake batter into the prepared tin and spread into an even layer. Bake for 35–40 minutes, or until the cake springs back to a light touch or a skewer inserted into the middle of the cake comes out clean.

Leave the cake to cool in the tin for about 15 minutes, before transferring it to a wire rack (using the parchment paper to lift it out) to cool completely.

For the frosting, it's very important that the butter and cream cheese are both at room temperature, otherwise it can be tricky to get the right texture. Place the butter and cream cheese into a large bowl and use an electric mixer to beat on medium-high speed for 2–3 minutes, or until smooth, creamy and fully combined. Add the icing sugar, salt and vanilla and mix on slow speed until the sugar has combined with the butter mixture, then mix on medium-high speed for 4–5 minutes, or until light and fluffy.

Spread the frosting all over the cooled cake, then sprinkle the desiccated coconut on top and serve.

This cake will keep for 2–3 days, but personally, I think it's best eaten within a day of frosting.

MATCHA ROLL CAKE

SERVES 8–10

One visit to Japan and I became obsessed with the baking, the ingredients and the apparent infatuation with all things matcha-flavoured. I saw a version of this cake in almost every department-store food hall, metro station bakery, and even all the brilliant convenience stores. Think of it as the Japanese version of the British Swiss roll. Similarly made with a whisked sponge cake, this version is based on chiffon cake – an incredibly soft and flexible sponge made with a little oil and milk. I have kept the flavours simple in line with what I ate in Japan with one small addition – a little white chocolate in the matcha whipped cream filling, which sweetens it just enough and makes for a creamier texture.

FOR THE MATCHA WHITE CHOCOLATE WHIPPED CREAM FILLING

240ml (8½fl oz/1 cup) double (heavy) cream

2 teaspoons matcha powder

50g (1¾oz) white chocolate, finely chopped

FOR THE MATCHA ROLL CAKE

40ml (1½fl oz/2 tablespoons + 2 teaspoons) neutral-tasting oil, plus extra for greasing

50ml (2fl oz/3 tablespoons + 1 teaspoon) whole milk

3 teaspoons matcha powder

3 large eggs, separated

¼ teaspoon cream of tartar

80g (2¾oz/⅓ cup + 1 tablespoon) caster (superfine) sugar

30g (1oz/¼ cup) plain (all-purpose) flour

30g (1oz/¼ cup) cornflour (cornstarch)

¼ teaspoon fine sea salt

Make the filling in advance as it needs a few hours to chill before use. Add a quarter of the cream to a small pan over a medium heat along with the matcha and whisk together to form a smooth paste. Whisk in the remaining cream, a little at a time to prevent the matcha from going lumpy, until fully combined. Bring the cream to a simmer, then immediately pour over the chocolate in a small, heatproof bowl and set aside for a couple of minutes before stirring to combine. Cover and refrigerate for at least 4 hours until cold.

Preheat the oven to 180°C (350°F), Gas Mark 4. Line the base of the baking tin with parchment paper. You can lightly grease the base of the tin to help the parchment paper stick, if you like, but ensure the sides remain clean, as we want the cake to cling to the sides of the tin as it bakes.

To make the roll cake, add the milk and matcha to a small pan and whisk together until smooth. Bring to a simmer over a medium heat, then remove from the heat and set aside.

Place the egg yolks into one bowl and the egg whites and cream of tartar into another. Add half of the sugar to the yolks, then, using an electric mixer, whisk for 3–4 minutes, or until pale and creamy. Add the oil and matcha milk and whisk briefly to combine. Add the flour, cornflour and salt, mix to form a smooth batter, then set aside.

Using the electric mixer (clean the whisk first), whisk the egg whites and cream of tartar on medium speed until foamy, then slowly sprinkle in the remaining sugar, a tablespoon at a time, whisking until the whites hold medium peaks.

The final meringue wants to be stiff but still flexible; if the mixture becomes over-whisked and dry, it will be hard to fold into the matcha mixture without losing volume.

Add the meringue to the matcha batter in three additions, gently folding together until streak-free, then pour into the prepared tin, gently levelling. Bake for 12–14 minutes or until the cake is lightly browned and springs back to a light touch.

Use a round-bladed knife to cut the cake away from the sides of the tin, then immediately invert the cake onto a sheet of parchment paper on a wire rack. While the cake is still warm, gently peel off the parchment paper from what is now the top of the cake. Leave to cool completely.

For the filling, transfer the cream mixture to a large bowl and whisk briefly until holding soft peaks. Spread over the cake, leaving the short edge near you clean, then carefully roll up the cake from this short edge. Refrigerate the cake, seam-side down, for a couple of hours before serving. The cake is very soft, so when cutting, it is best to use a serrated knife using a gentle sawing motion.

This cake is best served on the day it is made.

ROASTED PLUM ROLL CAKE

SERVES 12–14

This vertical roll cake is a fun but unusual way to create a round cake from a rectangular tin. If you have two 23 x 33cm (9 x 13in) baking tins, then you can go ahead and make the recipe in one go. If you only have one (how many of us have two, let's be real), you can divide the cake ingredients in half and make the layers one after the other. The purée can be prepared a couple of days in advance and stored in the fridge.

FOR THE ROASTED PLUM PURÉE

6 plums, halved and stones removed

1½ tablespoons light brown sugar

1½ tablespoons clear honey

juice of ½ lemon

whole spices, such as a few cardamom pods, a stick or two of cinnamon, a star anise or a couple of cloves (optional)

FOR THE CHIFFON ROLL CAKE

6 large eggs, separated

¼ teaspoon cream of tartar

160g (5¾oz/¾ cup + 1 tablespoon) caster (superfine) sugar

80ml (3fl oz/⅓ cup) neutral-tasting oil

100ml (3½fl oz/⅓ cup + 1 tablespoon + 1 teaspoon) whole milk

60g (2¼oz/½ cup) plain (all-purpose) flour

60g (2¼oz/½ cup) cornflour (cornstarch)

½ teaspoon fine sea salt

First, roast the plums. Preheat the oven to 180°C (350°F), Gas Mark 4. Place them, cut-side up, into the baking tin, scatter over the sugar, then drizzle over the honey and lemon juice. If you want to add a back note of spice to the plums, you can throw in whole spices. Bake for 20 minutes or until the fruit is a little squishy.

Once the plums are nice and soft, tip them and all the juices into a large jug so that the spices are fully submerged – they will continue to infuse. Once cooled, remove any spices and then use a stick blender to purée the fruit until smooth. If you don't want any little pieces in the buttercream, sieve it. Set the purée aside and wash the baking tin.

Line the base of the baking tin with parchment paper. You can lightly grease the base of the tin to help the parchment paper stick, if you like, but ensure the sides remain clean, as we want the cake to cling to the sides of the tin as it bakes.

Make the roll cake. Place the egg yolks into one bowl and the egg whites and cream of tartar into another. Add half of the sugar to the yolks and whisk together using an electric mixer for 3–4 minutes, or until pale, creamy and thick. Add the oil and milk and whisk briefly to combine. Add the flour, cornflour and salt, and mix to form a smooth batter. Set aside. Using the electric mixer (clean the whisk first), whisk the egg whites and cream of tartar on medium speed until foamy, then sprinkle in the remaining sugar, a tablespoon at a time, whisking until the whites hold medium peaks – you want the final meringue to be stiff but still flexible.

Add the meringue to the cake batter in three additions, gently folding until it's streak-free, then divide the batter between the prepared tins, gently levelling out.

Bake for 12–14 minutes or until each cake is lightly browned and springs back to a light touch. Use a round-bladed knife to cut the cakes away from the sides of the tins, then invert each cake on to a sheet of parchment paper. While still warm, gently peel off the lining paper and set aside to cool.

340g (11¾oz/3 sticks) unsalted butter, at room temperature, diced, plus extra for greasing

3 large egg whites (about 120ml/4fl oz /½ cup)

225g (8oz/1⅛ cups) caster (superfine) sugar

¼ teaspoon cream of tartar

1 teaspoon vanilla bean paste

TO DECORATE (OPTIONAL)

100g (3½oz) white chocolate, melted and cooled

2 tablespoons finely chopped pistachios

Make the buttercream. Place the egg whites, sugar and cream of tartar into a large, heatproof bowl set over a pan of simmering water (ensuring the bottom of the bowl doesn't touch the water underneath) and cook, whisking gently, until the sugar has dissolved (rub a bit of the mixture between your fingers and if there are sugar grains, cook a little longer). Remove the bowl from the heat and whisk using an electric mixer until the meringue is cooled, glossy and holding stiff peaks. Gradually add the butter, whisking until you have a thick buttercream texture, then whisk in the vanilla and 160ml (5½fl oz/⅔ cup) of the plum purée until combined.

To assemble the cake, trim the edges of the two cakes, then cut each cake in half lengthways to create four long strips. Brush each with a little of the remaining plum purée, then top with a thin layer of the buttercream. Working with one strip at a time, roll up from the short side like a Swiss roll, then line it up with the next strip and continue to roll up, continuing the roll with the remaining two strips to make one single cake.

Place the cake, swirl-side facing up, on a plate and cover the top and sides with the remaining buttercream. Chill in the refrigerator until the buttercream is firm. If decorating with white chocolate and pistachios, pour the melted chocolate on top of the chilled cake, teasing it toward the edge and allowing it to drip down the sides. Sprinkle over the pistachios. Leave to set for 20 minutes, then serve.

This cake is best served within 1–2 days of baking.

CLASSIC BIRTHDAY CAKE

SERVES 12–16

It's the law, birthday cake needs to include both chocolate and sprinkles, lots of sprinkles. When I was little, the birthday cake of choice was a simple cocoa affair topped with melted milk chocolate and decorations made from Smarties, chocolate fingers and any other candy desired that year. This recipe feels like another of those classic cakes, a simple yellow cake base and a chocolate fudge frosting. As this is not a layer cake, the fudge frosting doesn't need to be thick enough to hold a second cake layer. It's silky and smooth and stays that way, it won't harden over time.

FOR THE SHEET CAKE

170g (6oz/1½ sticks) unsalted butter, at room temperature, plus extra for greasing

320g (11¼oz/2½ cups + 1 tablespoon) plain (all-purpose) flour

3 teaspoons baking powder

½ teaspoon fine sea salt

350g (12oz/1¾ cups) caster (superfine) sugar

3 large eggs

2 teaspoons vanilla extract

175ml (6fl oz/⅔ cup + 1 tablespoon) sour cream

FOR THE CHOCOLATE FUDGE FROSTING

340g (11¾oz/3 sticks) unsalted butter, at room temperature

120g (4¼oz/1 cup) icing (powdered) sugar

2 tablespoons golden syrup or clear honey

60g (2¼oz/½ cup) cocoa powder

80ml (2¾fl oz/⅓ cup) hot water

80ml (2¾fl oz/⅓ cup) sour cream

1 teaspoon vanilla extract

200g (7oz) dark chocolate (70% cocoa solids), melted and cooled

sprinkles of your choice, to decorate

Preheat the oven to 180°C (350°F), Gas Mark 4. Lightly grease the baking tin and line the base with a piece of parchment paper.

For the cake, place the flour, baking powder and salt into a large bowl and whisk briefly to combine. Add the butter and sugar to a separate large bowl and, using an electric mixer, beat together on medium-high speed for about 5 minutes until light and fluffy. Add the eggs, one at a time, beating until fully combined before adding another. Add the vanilla and mix briefly to combine. Add the flour mixture in three additions, alternating with the sour cream, starting and finishing with the flour. Scrape the batter into the prepared tin and level out.

Bake for 35–40 minutes or until the cake springs back to a light touch. Leave to cool in the tin.

For the fudge frosting, place the butter in a large bowl and use an electric mixer to beat on high speed for a couple of minutes or until creamy and smooth. Add the sugar, golden syrup (or honey) and cocoa powder and beat on high speed for 5 minutes or until light and fluffy. Add the hot water, sour cream and vanilla to a small jug and whisk together. Add the sour cream mixture to the bowl and mix on medium speed until combined. It will look separated for a while but will come back together as a smooth frosting. Add the melted chocolate and beat briefly until smooth and silky.

Spread the frosting over the cake, finishing with a generous amount of sprinkles, which as far as I am concerned are mandatory. Cut into squares to serve.

Store in a sealed container for up to 3 days.

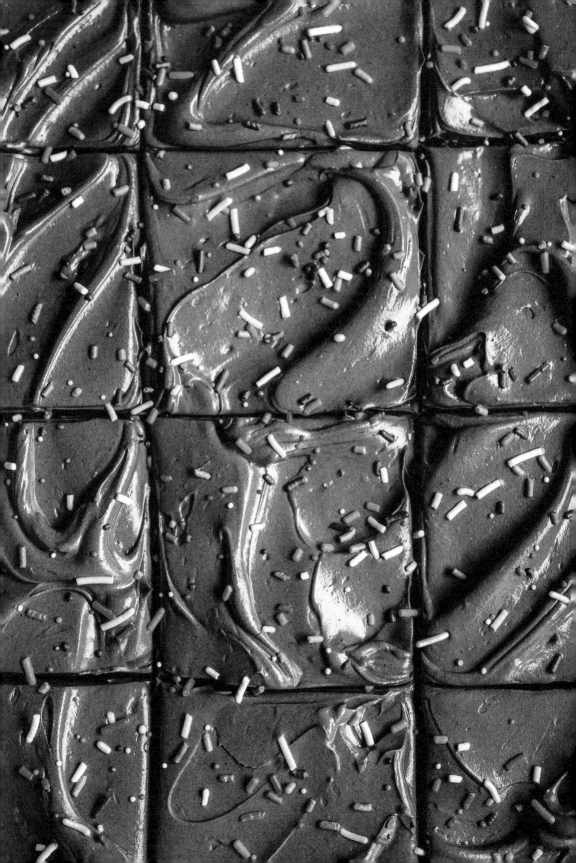

BLUEBERRY CORNMEAL BUCKLE

SERVES 12–15

A buckle is a glorious thing, a cake laced with fruit and topped with streusel. The name likely comes from the fact that as the cake bakes it buckles under the weight of the fruit and streusel. Regardless of where the name originates, it's a moist cake, almost in the same vein as coffee cake, and similarly, it's a not-too-sweet choice that is perfect with a mug of coffee or, with this particular recipe, a mug of tea.

FOR THE STREUSEL TOPPING

125g (4½oz/1⅓ cups) ground almonds

125g (4½oz/1⅓ cups + 1 tablespoon) oat flour

3 tablespoons caster (superfine) sugar

¼ teaspoon fine sea salt

100g (3½oz/7 tablespoons) unsalted butter, diced

FOR THE ALMOND CORNMEAL CAKE

185g (6½oz/1½ sticks + 1 tablespoon) unsalted butter, at room temperature, plus extra for greasing

250g (9oz/1¼ cups) caster (superfine) sugar

finely grated zest of 2 lemons

185g (6½oz/1¼ cups) fine cornmeal

185g (6½oz/1¾ cups + 3 tablespoons) ground almonds

¾ teaspoon baking powder

½ teaspoon fine sea salt

5 large eggs

2 teaspoons vanilla extract

450g (1lb) fresh blueberries

Preheat the oven to 180°C (350°F), Gas Mark 4. Lightly grease the baking tin and line with a piece of parchment paper that overhangs the two long sides of the tin, securing in place with metal clips.

To make the streusel topping, mix together the ground almonds, oat flour, sugar and salt, then rub in the butter using your fingertips until it resembles breadcrumbs. Pop this bowl into the freezer while you finish the cake batter.

For the cake, place the butter, sugar and lemon zest into a large bowl and beat together using an electric mixer for about 5 minutes or until light and fluffy.

Mix together the cornmeal, ground almonds, baking powder and salt in a separate bowl. Add the eggs to the butter mixture, one at a time, beating until fully combined before adding another. Add the vanilla and mix briefly to combine. Add the cornmeal mixture and mix together to form a smooth cake batter, then gently fold in the blueberries.

Pour the batter into the prepared baking tin and spread into an even layer, then sprinkle the chilled streusel mixture evenly over the top. Bake for 40–45 minutes or until a skewer inserted into the middle of the cake comes out clean.

Leave the cake to cool in the tin for about 20 minutes, before transferring it to a wire rack to cool completely. Once cool, cut into portions and serve.

Store in a sealed container for 2–3 days.

RASPBERRY CREAM LAMINGTONS

MAKES 20

Normally, my recipes are inspired by bakes I've tried on my travels. This recipe, however, was inspired by my brother's trips to Australia. He had an unusual version of the classic lamington at the bakery Flour and Stone in Sydney that had been soaked in a sweetened milk mixture, akin to a panna cotta. I loved this idea and so this is my impression of a cake I have never actually tried.

FOR THE SPONGE CAKE

30g (1oz/2 tablespoons) unsalted butter, plus extra for greasing

30ml (1fl oz/⅛ cup) whole milk

5 large eggs

185g (6½oz/¾ cup + 3 tablespoons) caster (superfine) sugar

185g (6½oz/1½ cups) self-raising flour, plus extra for dusting

¼ teaspoon fine sea salt

FOR THE VANILLA CREAM SOAK

2 sheets gelatine

400ml (14fl oz/1⅔ cups) double (heavy) cream

200ml (7fl oz/¾ cup + 1 tablespoon) whole milk

75g (2¾oz/¼ + ⅛ cups) caster (superfine) sugar

1 teaspoon vanilla bean paste

FOR THE COATING

320g (11¼oz/1 cup) raspberry jam

250g (9oz/3 cups) desiccated coconut

Preheat the oven to 180°C (350°F), Gas Mark 4. Lightly grease the baking tin, then line with a piece of parchment paper that overhangs the two long sides, securing in place with metal clips. Lightly grease the parchment paper and then dust the inside of the tin with flour, tapping out any excess.

To make the cake, first heat the butter and milk together, just until the butter has melted, then set aside. Place the eggs and sugar in a large bowl and, using an electric mixer, whisk on medium-high speed for 6–8 minutes, or until tripled in volume. When the whisk is lifted from the bowl the batter should leave a slowly dissolving ribbon on the surface.

Sift together the flour and salt, then in three additions, sift this over the egg mixture, folding together gently until the flour is incorporated, keeping the mixture as light as possible. Mix a large spoonful into the melted butter mixture, then add it to the remaining batter, gently folding together. Pour the batter into the prepared baking tin and gently level out.

Bake for 25–30 minutes or until the cake is golden brown and springs back to a gentle touch. Set aside to cool in the tin while you make the vanilla cream soak.

Add the gelatine to a bowl of ice-cold water and set aside for a few minutes to soften. Put the cream and milk into a small pan with the sugar and vanilla and bring to a simmer to dissolve the sugar, then remove from the heat. Squeeze out any excess water from the soaked gelatine, then add it to the hot cream mixture, stirring until dissolved. While the cake is still warm, poke it all over with a sharp knife and then slowly pour over the cream soak. Set aside for an hour, then cover with clingfilm and refrigerate overnight.

The next day, remove the cake from the tin and cut into 20 squares. For the coating, place the jam and 60ml (4 tablespoons /¼ cup) water into a small saucepan and bring to a simmer, stirring until smooth. Pour into a wide, shallow bowl, placing the coconut in another bowl. Dip each cake square into the jam, coating each side, then place into the coconut to coat each side. Transfer to a plate, then serve.

Store in a sealed container for up to 4 days.

CHOCOLATE AND CARDAMOM CARROT CAKE WITH BROWN BUTTER CREAM CHEESE FROSTING

SERVES 12–14

For the last 10 years my brother-in-law has badgered me to put a chocolate orange carrot cake into one of my books. I have, for those same 10 years, joked that I think it sounds awful. The truth is it was more fun to wind him up than admit it would work, so it's time to end the joke and give him a recipe for it. My interpretation has vaguely Scandi spicing and the best brown butter cream cheese frosting you've ever had, tasting like a toasty rich caramel.

FOR THE CARROT CAKE

300g (10½oz/2⅓ cups + 1 tablespoon) plain (all-purpose) flour

2 teaspoons baking powder

½ teaspoon fine sea salt

2 teaspoons ground cinnamon

1 teaspoon ground cardamom

zest of 2 oranges, juice of 1

300g (10½oz) carrots, grated

75g (2¾oz/½ cup) dark chocolate chips

150g (5½oz/1 cup) raisins or sultanas

4 large eggs

400g (14oz/2 cups) light brown sugar

240ml (8½fl oz/1 cup) light olive oil, plus extra for greasing

FOR THE TOPPING

1 batch cream cheese frosting (page 22)

milk chocolate shavings

finely grated zest of 1 orange

Preheat the oven to 180°C (350°F), Gas Mark 4. Lightly grease the baking tin, then line with a piece of parchment paper that overhangs the two long sides.

Place the flour, baking powder, salt, ground spices and orange zest into a large bowl and whisk together to combine. Add the carrots, chocolate chips and raisins. In a separate bowl, whisk together the eggs, sugar, olive oil and juice from 1 orange, mixing until combined. Pour the wet mixture in the bowl with the flour and stir together until everything is combined. Pour the cake batter into the prepared tin and spread into an even layer.

Bake for 35–40 minutes, or until the cake springs back to a light touch or a skewer inserted into the middle comes out clean.

Leave to cool in the tin for 20 minutes, then use the lining paper to carefully lift and transfer the cake to a wire rack to cool completely.

Make the cream cheese frosting according to the instructions on page 22, but first brown the butter. Place the butter into a small saucepan over a medium heat, stirring frequently. As the butter cooks it will first melt and then sizzle, splatter and then start to foam with little brown flecks. Pour into a bowl and refrigerate, stirring occasionally, until the butter is firm. Remove from the refrigerator and beat with an electric mixer, on its own, until soft and creamy. Proceed with the cream cheese frosting method as written on page 22. Spread over the top of the cake and finish with a grating of milk chocolate and the zest of another orange, if you like.

Kept covered, this cake will keep for 3–4 days.

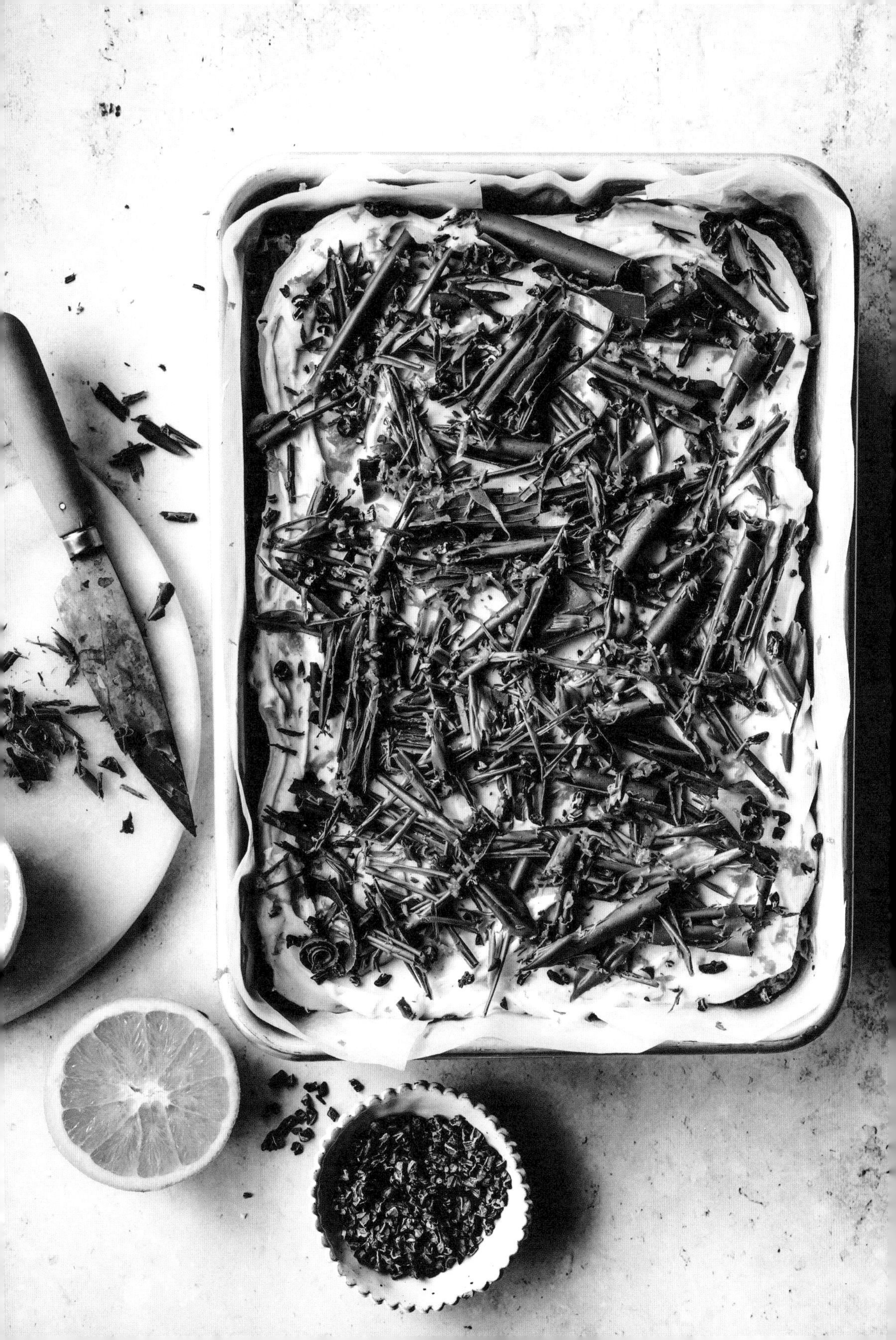

UPSIDE-DOWN BANANA AND BUCKWHEAT CAKE

SERVES 10–12

While banana bread is a useful recipe for forgotten overripe bananas, this isn't a cake for them. This is a banana cake you plan for, one you make if you think banana bread doesn't use enough bananas. The cake portion of this recipe isn't quite banana bread, it's lighter and its banana flavour isn't quite as strong, so this is where the banana topping comes into play. While you could use the cake portion of this recipe to make a layer cake or top simply with cream cheese frosting, this upside-down cake, with its sticky layer of caramel, is my favourite way to use it.

FOR THE BANANA TOPPING

75g (2¾oz/5 tablespoons) unsalted butter, plus extra for greasing

150g (5½oz/⅔ cup) light brown sugar

½ teaspoon vanilla bean paste

4–5 medium bananas

FOR THE BUCKWHEAT CAKE

150g (5½oz/1 cup + 1 tablespoon) plain (all-purpose) flour

3 teaspoons baking powder

½ teaspoon fine sea salt

2 small bananas, peeled (about 150g/5½oz)

120g (4¼oz/1 stick + ½ tablespoon) unsalted butter, at room temperature

125g (4½oz/½ cup + 1 tablespoon) light brown sugar

125g (4½oz/½ cup + 2 tablespoons) caster (superfine) sugar

3 large eggs

2 teaspoons vanilla extract

125ml (4fl oz/½ cup + 2 tablespoons) buttermilk

100g (3½oz/¾ cup + 1 teaspoon) buckwheat flour

NOTE Buckwheat doesn't like being mixed for too long, it can behave unusually and lead to heavy, dense cakes.

Preheat the oven to 180°C (350°F), Gas Mark 4. Lightly grease the baking tin and line the base with a piece of parchment paper.

Place all the ingredients for the topping, except the bananas, into a medium-sized saucepan and cook over a medium heat, stirring continuously, until everything has melted and you have a smooth sauce. Immediately pour into the prepared tin and spread into an even layer.

Peel and slice the bananas in half lengthways, then place them in the tin on top of the caramel. To fill in the gaps, you may need to cut one into smaller pieces to complete the jigsaw puzzle of the upside-down cake. Set aside.

For the cake, combine the plain flour, baking powder and salt in a mixing bowl. Mash the bananas in another bowl until no large lumps remain. Place the butter and both sugars into a large bowl using an electric mixer. Beat together on medium speed for about 5 minutes, or until the mixture is pale and fluffy.

Add the eggs, one at a time, beating until fully combined before adding another. Add the vanilla and mix briefly to combine. Add the plain flour mixture in three additions, alternating with the buttermilk, starting and finishing with the flour. Add the buckwheat flour and gently fold in using a spatula. Finally, fold in the mashed bananas. Scrape into the tin and spread over the bananas and caramel in an even layer.

Bake for 35–40 minutes or until golden brown and the centre of the cake springs back when gently pressed. Remove from the oven and cool in the tin for 10 minutes before inverting it on to a wire rack.

This will keep in a sealed container for a couple of days, but this really is a cake you make for a crowd, so it's best served warm and fresh from the oven.

OLIVE OIL CHERRY SNACK CAKE

SERVES 12

Snack cakes fall into a random sub-category of cakes that you wouldn't necessarily serve for a birthday or as dessert, think elevenses instead. They should be incredibly easy to bake, requiring nothing more than the simplest of icing sugar glazes, if anything at all. This is not a place for frosting or ganache, these are humble cakes that are perfect for a mid-morning sweet snack. This cherry version is made with an olive oil almond cake and topped with a mixture of cherries; I tend to use a couple of different varieties of sweet cherries in recipes like this, something like a classic Bing, and then if I can get them, I will also use Rainier (or Napoleon, which are very similar).

FOR THE OLIVE OIL CHERRY SNACK CAKE

3 large eggs

175g (6oz/¾ cup + 2 tablespoons) caster (superfine) sugar

finely grated zest of 2 lemons

120ml (4fl oz/½ cup) olive oil, plus extra for greasing

120ml (4fl oz/½ cup) natural yogurt

1 teaspoon vanilla extract

140g (5oz/1⅛ cup) plain (all-purpose) flour

100g (3½oz/1 cup) ground almonds

1½ teaspoons baking powder

1 teaspoon fine sea salt

300g (10½oz) fresh cherries, pitted and halved

2–3 tablespoons flaked almonds

FOR THE CHERRY ALMOND GLAZE

5 fresh cherries, pitted, or 2 tablespoons cherry juice

125g (4½oz/1 cup + 1 tablespoon) icing sugar

¼ teaspoon almond extract

pinch of fine sea salt

few drops of pink food colouring

Preheat the oven to 180°C (350°F), Gas Mark 4. Lightly grease your baking tin and line with a piece of parchment paper that overhangs the two long sides of the tin to make removing the cake easier later, securing in place with metal clips.

For the cake, add the eggs, sugar and lemon zest to a large bowl, then use an electric mixer to whisk for a minute or two until the sugar has fully dissolved. Continuing to whisk, pour in the olive oil and whisk for a minute or until slightly thickened, then briefly whisk in the yogurt and vanilla until fully combined. Add the flour, ground almonds, baking powder and salt and whisk briefly until you have a smooth cake batter. Pour this into the prepared baking tin, spreading evenly, then scatter over the cherries and flaked almonds.

Bake for 35 minutes or until the cake is golden brown and feels firm to the touch. Leave the cake to cool in the tin for 15–20 minutes, before using the parchment paper to carefully lift it out on to a wire rack to cool completely.

Once fully cooled, you can either serve the cake with a light dusting of icing sugar or you can make a simple cherry glaze.

For the glaze, purée the cherries, then pass them through a fine sieve. Mix together 2 tablespoons of the purée (or the juice, if using) and the icing sugar in a small bowl until smooth. Add the almond extract, salt and enough food colouring to make a pale pink glaze. Drizzle liberally over the cake, then serve.

Store in a sealed container for 2 days.

BARS & COOKIES

TURTLE BROWNIES

MAKES 12–20, DEPENDING ON DESIRED SIZE

When it comes to brownies I am a purist. No nuts, no fruit, I want pure unadulterated chocolate. There is, however, the rarest of occasions when I am willing to break these self-imposed rules and that would be when caramel is involved. For the uninitiated, a 'turtle' is a classic confection made of chocolate, pecans and caramel, and let's be honest, if there is one thing that makes brownies better, it's the addition of caramel.

FOR THE RYE CHOCOLATE BROWNIES

200g (7oz/1¾ sticks) unsalted butter, diced, plus extra for greasing

175g (6oz/1¾ cups) wholemeal rye flour

50g (1¾oz/⅔ cup) cocoa powder

½ teaspoon flaked sea salt

½ teaspoon baking powder

300g (10½oz) dark chocolate (65–75% cocoa solids), roughly chopped

150g (5½oz/¾ cup) caster (superfine) sugar

220g (8oz/1 cup) light brown sugar

4 large eggs

1 teaspoon vanilla extract

80g (2¾oz/⅔ cup) pecans, roughly chopped

50g (1¾oz) milk chocolate, roughly chopped (or chocolate chips)

FOR THE SALTED CARAMEL

100g (3½oz/½ cup) caster (superfine) sugar

80ml (3fl oz/⅓ cup) double (heavy) cream

15g (½oz/1 tablespoon) unsalted butter

¼ teaspoon flaked sea salt, plus extra for sprinkling (optional)

NOTE You can substitute the rye for plain (all-purpose) flour, but if you haven't tried rye I would implore you to, it makes a very special brownie.

Preheat the oven to 180°C (350°F), Gas Mark 4. Lightly grease the baking tin and line with a piece of parchment paper that goes up the sides of the tin.

For the brownies, sift the flour, cocoa, salt and baking powder into a large bowl and set aside. Place the butter and dark chocolate in a heatproof bowl and set over a pan of simmering water (ensuring the bottom of the bowl doesn't touch the water underneath), stirring occasionally, until fully melted. Remove from the heat and set aside.

Place both sugars, the eggs and vanilla into a separate large bowl and, using an electric mixer, whisk together on medium-high speed for 4–5 minutes, or until increased in volume, thick and pale. This gives the brownies a fudgy texture and a thin crackly crust. Turn the mixer to low speed, pour in the chocolate mixture and mix until combined.

Fold the dry ingredients into the chocolate mixture using a spatula until just the odd fleck of flour remains. Scrape into the prepared tin and spread evenly. Sprinkle over half the pecans and half the milk chocolate pieces/chips.

Bake for 25 minutes, or until a toothpick inserted comes out with moist crumbs. Leave to cool in the tin. Chill for a couple of hours in the refrigerator for a fudgier brownie.

For the salted caramel, place the sugar in a small saucepan and cook over a medium heat until melted and the colour of an old copper coin. Add the cream, butter and salt. Once the bubbling has subsided, if there are any lumps, reduce the heat and stir until melted. Pour the caramel into a small, heatproof bowl and set aside for 10–15 minutes until slightly thickened.

To finish, drizzle the caramel over the brownies and sprinkle over the remaining pecans and milk chocolate. Scatter over a little extra flaked sea salt if you're a fan of sweet and salty. Remove from the tin and cut into squares.

Store in a sealed container for 4 days.

SWEET AND SALTY RICE CRISPY TREATS

MAKES 24 BARS

Who said rice crispy treats are just for kids? These sweet and salty bars are a spin on the classic rice crispy treats and I would happily have them on my birthday as a fully grown adult. Made with brown butter for a more flavourful base, the bars are also packed full of sweet and salty goodies to make a very simple and very moreish bake. You can use any of your favourite sweet and salty treats, so for me that means pretzels, peanuts and a healthy dose of milk chocolate, but feel free to use your imagination for your own version.

170g (6oz/1½ sticks) unsalted butter, diced, plus extra for greasing

¼ teaspoon flaked sea salt

400g (14oz) mini marshmallows

200g (7oz/8 cups) crisped/toasted rice cereal (Rice Krispies)

70g (2½oz/1½ cups) salted pretzels

70g (2½oz/½ cup) salted peanuts, halved

170g (6oz) milk chocolate, roughly chopped

4 tablespoons cocoa nibs

Lightly grease the baking tin and line with a large sheet of parchment paper that goes up the sides of the tin.

Melt the butter in a large saucepan over a medium heat until it browns, stirring frequently. The butter will melt, then sizzle and splatter and then start to foam. As it foams, you'll see little golden brown flecks start to appear. Before these flecks burn, add the salt and marshmallows and reduce the heat to low. Stir until the marshmallows have melted and the mixture is smooth and combined.

Pour the marshmallow mixture into a large, heatproof bowl containing the rice cereal and stir to combine. Add all the remaining ingredients (reserving a small handful of each for the topping) and quickly stir to combine – this is a very sticky mixture and as it cools it will be harder to work with, so stir quickly.

Turn the mixture into the prepared tin and, using lightly oiled hands, press into an even layer. Sprinkle over the reserved ingredients and gently press into the marshmallow mixture. Leave to set at room temperature for about 4 hours.

To serve, turn the mixture out of the tin in one piece and then use a large, serrated knife to cut it into 24 bars.

Store in a sealed container for up to 3 days.

NOTE I like to use white marshmallows for their lack of colour, and mini marshmallows as they melt a little more easily, but any marshmallows will work in this recipe.

PEANUT BUTTER BROOKIES

MAKES 12–24, DEPENDING ON DESIRED SIZE

What's better than a brownie? A brownie with a layer of peanut butter cookie, that's what. While you are technically making two recipes for just one dish, both are quick and easy and, trust me, these brownies are worth the little extra effort. The beauty of this dish (other than its flavours) is the textures, as the brownie is tender and fudgy, packed full of rich chocolate flavour, while the cookie is chewy and just a little bit salty from the peanuts, which really helps amp up the peanut flavour. As there is so much going on in this, I prefer to cut it into smaller pieces, 24 pieces per recipe, but you can serve these as normal brownies, so 12 pieces per recipe.

FOR THE PEANUT BUTTER COOKIE LAYER

160g (5¾oz/½ cup + 2 tablespoons) smooth peanut butter

220g (8oz/1 cup) light brown sugar

1 large egg, plus 2 large egg yolks

100g (3½oz/¾ cup) plain (all-purpose) flour

1 teaspoon bicarbonate of soda

½ teaspoon fine sea salt

100g (3oz) salted peanuts, roughly chopped

FOR THE BROWNIE LAYER

150g (5½oz/1⅓ sticks) unsalted butter, diced, plus extra for greasing

85g (3oz/1 cup) cocoa powder

100g (3½oz/½ cup) caster (superfine) sugar

100g (3½oz/⅓ cup + 2 tablespoons) light brown sugar

¼ teaspoon fine sea salt

1 teaspoon vanilla extract

2 large eggs

70g (2½oz/½ cup + 1 tablespoon) plain (all-purpose) flour

Preheat the oven to 180°C (350°F), Gas Mark 4. Lightly grease the baking tin and line with a piece of parchment paper that overhangs the two long sides. Secure in place with metal clips.

For the peanut butter cookie layer, mix the peanut butter and brown sugar together in a large bowl for a couple of minutes until combined and slightly lightened. Add the egg and egg yolks and beat together for a further 2–3 minutes. Add all the remaining ingredients (reserving 3 tablespoons of the peanuts for sprinkling over later) and gently mix together to form a uniform cookie dough. Spread the cookie dough in an even layer in the prepared tin, then set aside.

For the brownie layer, add the butter and cocoa to a small saucepan over a medium heat, stirring constantly, until melted and smooth. Remove from the heat and set aside. Place the sugars, salt, vanilla and eggs in a large bowl and whisk together with an electric mixer for 2–3 minutes or until slightly thickened and pale. Pour in the melted butter mixture, mixing briefly until combined, then fold in the flour. Pour the batter over the cookie layer and spread into an even layer, then sprinkle over the reserved peanuts.

Bake for about 25–30 minutes, or until a skewer inserted into the middle comes out with a few moist crumbs.

Leave the brookies to cool completely in the tin, before using the parchment paper to lift them from the tin and cutting into squares.

Store in a sealed container for 3–4 days.

ANZAC CARAMEL CHOCOLATE SLICES

MAKES 20

Anzac Cookies? Love them! Millionaire's Shortbread? Grew up eating them. But what happens when you mash the two together? Utterly wonderful, joyous things, that's what. When making the caramel, ignore your phone for a minute; Instagram® can wait, the caramel needs your total and undivided attention. Anzac cookies, if you haven't come across them, are Antipodean favourites originally made to raise money to support the war effort in the First World War.

FOR THE ANZAC BASE

85g (3oz/⅔ cup) plain (all-purpose) flour

60g (2¼oz/¾ cup) rolled oats

40g (1½oz/½ cup) desiccated coconut

¼ teaspoon flaked sea salt

75g (2¾oz/⅔ stick) unsalted butter

2 tablespoons golden syrup or clear honey

100g (3½oz/½ cup – 2 teaspoons) light brown sugar

¼ teaspoon bicarbonate of soda

FOR THE CARAMEL FILLING

150g (5½oz/1⅓ sticks) unsalted butter

397g (14oz) can condensed milk

3 tablespoons golden syrup or clear honey

110g (4oz/½ cup) light brown sugar

FOR THE TOPPING

200g (7oz) dark chocolate, melted

flaked sea salt, for sprinkling (optional)

NOTE If you have an instant-read thermometer, the caramel, when ready, should reach 112°C/235°F.

Preheat the oven to 180°C (350°F), Gas Mark 4. Line the baking tin with a piece of parchment paper that overhangs the two long sides of the tin, securing in place with metal clips.

To make the base, combine the flour, oats, coconut and salt in a large bowl. Place the butter, golden syrup or honey and sugar in a saucepan and cook over a medium heat, stirring every now and then, until melted. Remove from the heat and add the bicarbonate of soda and 1 tablespoon of water, stirring together for a minute until the mixture is a little foamy. Pour this over the oat mixture and mix together until well combined. While the Anzac mixture is still warm, tip it into the prepared tin and press into a flat and even layer.

Bake for 20–25 minutes, or until golden brown and a little darker around the edges. Leave to cool in the tin while you make the caramel.

Add all the caramel filling ingredients to a medium-sized saucepan and cook, stirring constantly, until the mixture comes to a simmer. Reduce the heat to low and continue to stir, scraping the bottom of the pan regularly to prevent catching, for 10–15 minutes, until the mixture has thickened and darkened a shade or two. Remove from the heat and pour the caramel over the base. This mixture is very hot, so ease it into the corners by lifting and tilting the tin as needed. Set aside to cool for 30 minutes.

For the topping, pour the melted chocolate over the caramel and use an offset spatula to spread it out evenly. Pop the tin in the refrigerator and leave for a couple of hours to allow everything to fully set (if you want to sprinkle with sea salt, allow the chocolate to turn a little tacky before sprinkling, otherwise it will sink into the chocolate).

To serve, remove from the tin using the parchment paper and cut into squares. I keep these in the refrigerator, as the chocolate isn't tempered, but I allow them to come to room temperature before serving as the textures are at their best.

Store in a sealed container for 4–5 days.

TAHINI CHOCOLATE CHIP COOKIE BARS

MAKES 16

Chocolate chip cookies are a constant in my house, whether it is a batch resting in the freezer waiting for a cookie emergency, or it is a batch of these cookie bars for when I want to make cookies but prefer to skip the shaping and get these baked nice and fast – especially good for when friends come over unannounced. The tahini in this recipe adds a warm nuttiness that is more subtle than peanut butter, but adds a great depth of flavour that makes these cookie bars really sing.

100g (3½oz/7 tablespoons) unsalted butter, diced, plus extra for greasing

280g (10oz/2¼ cups) plain (all-purpose) flour

¾ teaspoon bicarbonate of soda (baking soda)

1 teaspoon flaked sea salt

75g (2¾oz/¼ cup) tahini

125g (4½oz/½ cup + 2 tablespoons) caster (superfine) sugar

125g (4½oz/½ cup + 1 tablespoon) light brown sugar

1 large egg, plus 1 large egg yolk

1 teaspoon vanilla extract

250g (9oz) dark chocolate, roughly chopped

Preheat the oven to 180°C (350°F), Gas Mark 4. Lightly grease the base of the baking tin, then line with a piece of parchment paper that overhangs the two long sides. Secure the paper in place with two metal clips.

Follow the method on page 47 to create browned butter.

Add the flour, bicarbonate of soda and salt to a separate bowl and whisk briefly to combine. Add the tahini and both sugars to the bowl of melted butter, then use an electric mixer to whisk everything together for about 5 minutes, until the mixture is combined and lightened. Add the egg, egg yolk and vanilla and mix briefly to combine. Add the flour mixture and gently mix until most of the flour has been absorbed, then stir in the chocolate until evenly distributed. Scrape the cookie dough into the prepared baking tin and gently press into an even layer.

Bake for 25–30 minutes, or until golden. Leave to cool completely in the tin. Use the parchment paper to lift the cookie mixture from the tin and then cut into squares using a large, sharp knife.

Store in a sealed container for 3–4 days.

NOTE For this recipe, I prefer to roughly chop bars of chocolate to get different-sized pieces, which gives a more interesting taste and texture to these. While I prefer to use a dark chocolate for this recipe, the tahini also pairs beautifully with milk chocolate, so use whatever you prefer.

GIANDUJA BLONDIES

MAKES 12–20, DEPENDING ON DESIRED SIZE

Italy has given the world many gourmet gifts, including a plethora of pasta and a scoop of gelato, so it's no wonder I love the country. But my real Italian love affair is with a confection invented out of necessity, a wartime treat that really has my heart. The story goes that in the 1800s Napoleon blocked France and its allies from trading with Britain, which had the disastrous effect of slowing the flow of cocoa into Italy. To bulk out the limited cacao available, chocolate makers ground it into chocolate bulked out with hazelnuts (which were plentiful) to make gianduja (a sweet chocolate-hazelnut paste). I don't have a chocolate mill at home to make my own, so instead I'm using the two flavours to make gianduja-inspired blondies.

200g (7oz/1¾ sticks) unsalted butter, plus extra for greasing

365g (12½oz/1⅔ cups) light brown sugar

2 large eggs, plus 4 large egg yolks

65g (2½oz/¼ cup) hazelnut butter (see Note)

1 tablespoon vanilla extract

200g (7oz/1½ cups + 1 tablespoon) plain (all-purpose) flour

1 teaspoon baking powder

½ teaspoon fine sea salt

200g (7oz) milk chocolate, roughly chopped

200g (7oz) hazelnuts, roughly chopped

NOTE This recipe includes hazelnut butter, which can be a little tricky to find (try health food shops or online). You can replace it with almond butter which won't give as much flavour but is a happy substitution. An equal amount of extra unsalted butter also works if you don't want to use a nut butter.

Preheat the oven to 190°C (375°F), Gas Mark 5. Lightly grease the baking tin and line with a piece of parchment paper that overhangs the two long sides of the tin, securing in place with metal clips.

Start by making the brown butter. Melt the butter in a small saucepan over a medium heat until it browns, stirring frequently. The butter will melt, then sizzle and splatter and then it will start to foam. As it foams, you'll see little golden brown flecks start to appear. Before these flecks burn, remove the pan from the heat, then pour into a large, heatproof bowl and cool for 5 minutes.

Next, add the sugar, eggs, egg yolks, hazelnut butter and vanilla to the melted butter and whisk together for 2–3 minutes or until combined. Add the remaining ingredients and gently mix together until combined. If you want a more decorative finish, you can reserve some of the chopped chocolate and hazelnuts to sprinkle over the blondie mixture before baking.

Pour the batter into the prepared tin and spread into an even layer (sprinkling any reserved ingredients over the top). Bake for about 30 minutes or until a skewer inserted in the middle of the blondies comes out with just a few moist crumbs attached.

Leave the blondies to cool completely in the tin before removing and cutting into squares.

Store in a sealed container for 4–5 days.

PEPPERMINT CHOCOLATE SLICES

MAKES 16

The combination of chocolate and peppermint is heavenly and this recipe, inspired by the Aussie mint slice, is a great way to show it off. Technically a refrigerator/icebox cake, it is incredibly easy to make, even if it has a couple of different elements to prepare.

FOR THE BASE

300g (10½oz) digestives or graham crackers

170g (6oz/1½ sticks) unsalted butter, diced

50g (1¾oz/⅔ cup) cocoa powder

75g (2¾oz/⅓ cup) light brown sugar

2 large eggs

1 teaspoon vanilla extract

150g (5½oz/1¾ cups) desiccated coconut

½ teaspoon flaked sea salt

FOR THE PEPPERMINT LAYER

85g (3oz/¾ stick) unsalted butter, at room temperature

330g (11½oz/2½ cups) icing (powdered) sugar

80ml (3fl oz/⅓ cup) double (heavy) cream

2 teaspoons peppermint extract

green food colouring (optional)

FOR THE CHOCOLATE TOPPING

225g (8oz) dark chocolate (60% cocoa solids), roughly chopped

40g (1½oz/3 tablespoons) unsalted butter

1 tablespoon golden syrup or clear honey

Lightly grease the baking tin, then line with a strip of parchment paper that overhangs the two long sides of the tin. Secure the paper in place with two metal clips.

To make the base, place the digestives or graham crackers into a large freezer bag and crush into crumbs using a rolling pin (a few small chunks are totally fine). Place the butter, cocoa and sugar into a heatproof bowl set over a pan of simmering water (ensuring the bottom of the bowl doesn't touch the water underneath) and stir until the butter is melted and everything is smooth. Add the eggs and whisk for a couple of minutes, or until the mixture thickens. Remove from the heat and mix in the remaining ingredients. Scrape into the prepared tin and spread into an even layer. Refrigerate while you make the peppermint layer.

For the peppermint layer, place the butter into a large bowl and, using an electric mixer, beat on medium speed, or until the butter is light and creamy. Slowly incorporate the sugar, then increase the speed to high and beat for about 5 minutes, or until light and fluffy. Pour in the cream and peppermint extract, plus a drop or two of food colouring (if using) and mix until evenly combined. Scrape into the tin, spreading over the base in an even layer. Refrigerate for an hour before making the topping.

Place all the topping ingredients in a heatproof bowl set over a pan of simmering water (ensuring the bottom of the bowl doesn't touch the water underneath) and stir occasionally until everything is melted and smooth. Remove from the heat and pour over the filling, spreading into an even layer. Refrigerate until set.

To serve, use the parchment paper to lift the mixture from the tin, then cut into pieces using a sharp knife. If you want clean slices, using a knife that's been heated in hot water (dried before using) for each cut will help.

Store in a sealed container in the refrigerator for up to a week.

RASPBERRY CHEESECAKE STREUSEL SQUARES

MAKES 16–24

Lemon-infused cheesecake bars topped with jammy raspberries would be wonderful just on their own, but I wanted to make something a little more impressive, so these are topped with oat streusel, adding great texture. While that might seem like you're having to make another element, you actually just make a bigger batch of the base, keeping back a small amount and crumbling it over the cheesecake. I like these with a big mug of tea, cutting them into small squares for a little sweet treat, but if you prefer, you can cut them into more regular brownie-sized pieces.

FOR THE STREUSEL

225g (8oz/2¾ cups) unsalted butter, melted, plus extra for greasing

350g (12oz/2 cups) plain (all-purpose) flour

200g (7oz/½ cup) caster (superfine) sugar

¼ teaspoon fine sea salt

4 tablespoons rolled oats

FOR THE CHEESECAKE

565g (1lb 4½oz) full-fat cream cheese, at room temperature

120ml (4fl oz/½ cup) sour cream, at room temperature

200g (7oz/1 cup) caster (superfine) sugar

2 tablespoons cornflour (cornstarch)

2 teaspoons vanilla bean paste

finely grated zest of 2 lemons

2 large eggs

FOR THE RASPBERRY FILLING

3 tablespoons raspberry jam

300g (10½oz) fresh raspberries

Preheat the oven to 180°C (350°F), Gas Mark 4. Lightly grease the baking tin, then line with a strip of parchment paper that overhangs the two long sides of the tin. Secure the paper in place with two metal clips.

For the streusel, mix together the flour, sugar and salt in a large bowl. Gradually drizzle in the melted butter, stirring with a fork to combine until the mixture has formed clumps, then tip about two-thirds of the mixture into the prepared tin and spread out evenly. Use a glass to compact it into a flat layer. Dock all over with a fork and then freeze for 10 minutes. Mix the remaining streusel with the oats and refrigerate until needed.

Bake the base for 20 minutes, or until just starting to brown, then remove and set aside.

To make the cheesecake, place all the ingredients into a large bowl and mix together until smooth and evenly combined. Pour the cheesecake mix evenly over the base.

For the filling, gently warm the jam in a pan until loose, then remove from the heat and mix with the raspberries, coating evenly. Dot the raspberry mixture over the cheesecake, then crumble the reserved streusel evenly over the top.

Bake for 35–40 minutes, or until the streusel is lightly browned.

Leave to cool in the tin for an hour, then refrigerate for at least 4 hours, before cutting into squares to serve.

Store in a sealed container in the refrigerator for 4 days.

S'MORE COOKIE BARS

MAKES 12

I'm British, so S'mores were not really part of my Scouting life when I was a child. Our campfire cookouts definitely included marshmallows roasted over an open fire and sandwiched between digestive biscuits, but there was a distinct lack of chocolate and a proper S'more needs chocolate. These bars are like a S'more when you don't really want to venture outside to start a fire but still want the warming nostalgia a roasted marshmallow can bring.

FOR THE BISCUIT BASE

170g (6oz/1½ sticks) unsalted butter, diced and chilled, plus extra for greasing

100g (3½oz) digestives or graham crackers

185g (6½oz/1½ cups + 1 teaspoon) plain (all-purpose) wholemeal flour

75g (2¾oz/¼ cup + 2 tablespoons) caster (superfine) sugar

FOR THE FILLING AND TOPPING

300g (10½oz) dark chocolate (60% cocoa solids), roughly chopped

300ml (10fl oz/1¼ cups) double (heavy) cream

1 teaspoon vanilla extract

pinch of fine sea salt

200g (7oz/4 cups) mini marshmallows

Preheat the oven to 180°C (350°F), Gas Mark 4. Lightly grease the baking tin, then line with a piece of parchment paper that overhangs the two long sides of the tin. Secure the paper in place with two metal clips.

For the base, add the digestives or graham crackers to a food processor and pulse a few times to break into crumbs with some little chunks remaining (we don't want a super fine powder), then tip into a bowl and set aside. Add the flour and sugar to the food processor and pulse to combine. Add the butter and pulse until the mixture just starts to clump together, then add the biscuit crumbs and pulse a couple of times to mix. Scrape the mixture into the prepared tin and use a glass to press it into a flat, even layer. Refrigerate for 20 minutes.

Bake the base for about 30 minutes, or until golden brown. Set aside to cool completely in the tin.

For the filling, place the chocolate into a heatproof bowl. Place the cream, vanilla and salt into a saucepan and bring to a simmer over a medium heat. Pour the hot cream over the chocolate and set aside for a couple of minutes, then stir to form a smooth, glossy ganache. Pour over the cooled base, spreading evenly. Refrigerate for at least an hour, or until the ganache is firm.

Scatter over the mini marshmallows in an even layer, trying to ensure the ganache is fully covered.

Preheat the grill (broiler) to high. Place the baking tin under the grill and cook until the marshmallows are as dark as you like (I want them almost burnt), but don't walk away as the marshmallows will toast quickly.

Set the bars aside at room temperature for 30 minutes to allow the marshmallows to cool.

Once cooled, lift out of the tin and place onto a chopping board (using the parchment paper to help). These can be a little messy to cut, so if you want neat slices, between each cut, dip the knife in hot water and wipe dry.

Store in a sealed container for 4 days.

MALTED CHOCOLATE TIFFIN

MAKES 16

I think it's possible that every kid of the '80s and maybe the '90s made tiffin as a child. It is the ultimate recipe to keep young hands busy for an hour during the summer holidays. Joyously unfussy with no real technique to speak of – it's basically melt and mix. For my version, I have kept things pretty much as they always are, but I've soaked the fruit in alcohol because I'm an adult now and it sounded good to me (but exclude this for children). I have also added a little hint of malt flavour, which is such a wonderful pairing with chocolate.

150g (5½oz/1⅓ stick) unsalted butter, plus extra for greasing

170g (6oz/1⅓ cups) raisins

4 tablespoons amaretto or rum (optional)

115g (4oz/⅓ cup) golden syrup or clear honey

1 teaspoon vanilla extract

½ teaspoon fine sea salt

170g (6oz) dark chocolate (70% cocoa solids), roughly chopped

170g (6oz) milk chocolate (35–40% cocoa solids), roughly chopped

3 tablespoons Ovaltine (see Note)

250g (9oz) malted biscuits, digestives or graham crackers, broken into small pieces

extra cocoa powder and/or melted white chocolate, to serve (optional)

Lightly grease the baking tin and line with a large piece of parchment paper that covers all the sides of the tin.

Place the raisins and alcohol (if using) into a small, heatproof bowl and microwave on high for 30-second bursts, stirring between each, until the alcohol has been almost entirely absorbed by the fruit. Set aside.

Place the butter, golden syrup (or honey), vanilla and salt into a large saucepan over a medium-low heat and cook, stirring occasionally, until melted and smooth. Add the two types of chocolate and the Ovaltine and stir constantly until melted. Remove the pan from the heat and add the biscuits and raisins, stirring so that everything is coated in chocolate. Scrape the mixture into the prepared tin and spread into an even layer. Refrigerate the tiffin for a few hours, or until firm.

To serve, remove the tiffin from the tin and cut into pieces. You can serve them as is, or you can give them a little flair and dust with cocoa or drizzle with a little melted white chocolate, or if you're like me, you can do both.

Store in a sealed container in the refrigerator for up to 4 days (the biscuit element will slowly soften over time).

NOTE If you can't find Ovaltine, you can use Horlicks or malt powder, but the flavour isn't as pronounced.

FIG ROLL BARS

MAKES 16

Fig rolls are perhaps old-fashioned and deeply uncool, something your grandma loves. Well, I will happily put my hand up and say I adore these. While my version is a bar, it manages to taste incredibly close to the packaged version, improving on the one element that you could argue is the original's downfall, with a moister and more flavourful crust.

FOR THE FILLING

400g (14oz) dried figs, roughly chopped

100g (3½oz/½ cup) caster (superfine) sugar

finely grated zest and juice of 1 large orange

1 teaspoon fennel seeds, finely ground

2 teaspoons ground mixed spice (or pumpkin pie spice blend)

FOR THE WHOLEMEAL DOUGH

315g (11oz/2½ cups) plain (all-purpose) flour, plus extra for dusting

140g (5oz/1 cup + 2 tablespoons) plain (all-purpose) wholemeal flour

150g (5½oz/¾ cup) caster (superfine) sugar

¼ teaspoon fine sea salt

250g (9oz/2 sticks + 2 tablespoons) unsalted butter, diced, plus extra for greasing

3 large egg yolks

3 tablespoons whole milk

demerara sugar, for sprinkling

First, make the filling. Place the figs into a medium-sized saucepan with 240ml (8½fl oz/1 cup) water, the sugar, orange zest and juice and spices. Cook over a medium heat until the water has almost entirely evaporated and the figs are softened. Scrape into a food processor and purée until smooth. Scrape into a bowl, cover and refrigerate until cold.

For the dough, place both flours, the sugar and salt into a clean food processor and pulse a few times to combine. Add the butter and pulse until the mixture resembles breadcrumbs. Then add two of the egg yolks and the milk and pulse until the mixture starts to clump together, then tip it out on to a work surface and use your hands to briefly work it into a uniform dough. Divide the dough in half, press each portion into a flat rectangle and wrap in clingfilm, then refrigerate for an hour or so until firm.

Lightly grease the baking tin, then line with a strip of parchment paper that overhangs the two long sides of the tin. Secure the paper in place with two metal clips.

Working with one piece of dough at a time, roll it out on a lightly floured work surface until just larger than the tin. Trim the dough into a neat 23 x 33cm (9 x 13in) rectangle so that it is a snug fit and carefully lift into the tin. Spread the fig filling over the pastry base, leaving a 1cm (½in) border around the outside, brushing the edge with a little water to dampen. Roll out and trim the second piece of dough, then carefully place it on top of the filling, pressing the edges together to seal. Use a knife to score into bars and then use a fork to dock a few vent holes in each bar. Refrigerate for 30 minutes before baking.

Preheat the oven to 190°C (375°F), Gas Mark 5.

To bake, lightly beat the remaining egg yolk with a splash of water and brush over the bars, then sprinkle with demerara sugar. Bake for 45–50 minutes, or until golden brown.

Leave to cool completely in the tin, then use a serrated knife to cut into bars.

Store in a sealed container for up to 3 days.

ALFAJORES BARS

MAKES 16

Dulce de leche, the South American condensed milk caramel, is one of the ingredients I keep in my storecupboard at all times. You can use it to whip up a whole host of quick desserts and, let's be real, eating it by the spoonful is also always an option. This recipe is a bar version of the Argentinean alfajores. Normally these cookies are made with a high proportion of cornflour so they are incredibly tender. As a bar cookie, I have included some cornflour, but if it was made entirely with cornflour it would be tricky to cut into bars, so these are more of a tender shortbread.

225g (8oz/2 sticks) unsalted butter at room temperature, plus extra for greasing

150g (5½oz/¾ cup) caster (superfine) sugar

300g (10½oz/2⅓ cups + 1 tablespoon) plain (all-purpose) flour

50g (⅓ cup + 1 tablespoon) cornflour (cornstarch)

¼ teaspoon fine sea salt

360g (12½oz/1 cup) dulce de leche

85g (3oz/1 cup) desiccated coconut (see Note)

Preheat the oven to 180°C (350°F), Gas Mark 4. Lightly grease the baking tin, then line with a strip of parchment paper that overhangs the two long sides of the tin. Secure the paper in place with two metal clips.

Place the butter and sugar into a large bowl and beat together using an electric mixer for about 3 minutes until light and creamy. Add the flour, cornflour and salt and mix on low speed just until everything comes together into a uniform dough. Remove about two-thirds of the dough and place in the prepared tin, pressing into an even layer. Spread over the dulce de leche. Add the coconut to the remaining cookie base and mix briefly to combine, then crumble this evenly over the dulce de leche.

Bake for 30–40 minutes, or until the topping is lightly browned. If the coconut is browning too quickly while baking, tent the tin with foil.

Leave the mixture to cool completely in the tin before transferring to the refrigerator for an hour. Once chilled, lift from the tin and cut into pieces. These are on the richer side, so you can cut them into 16 bars as suggested, or into smaller pieces to serve a crowd.

Store in a sealed container for 2–3 days.

NOTE It is best to use un-toasted coconut as it is likely to catch during baking if it's pre-toasted. You can use either desiccated or dried coconut flakes, or as I prefer, a mix of the two.

WHOLEMEAL BROWN BUTTER APRICOT CRUMBLE BARS

MAKES 12

These bars are so simple that it's all the more important to use good-quality ingredients. Don't make this unless your apricots are already delicious, because a little sugar and lemon zest won't be enough to hide sad and out of season fruit. To give a little gentle hug to the apricots, the fruit is surrounded by a shortbread-style dough made with brown butter and wholemeal flour, nothing too extravagant but just enough to really make these special.

FOR THE BROWN BUTTER SHORTBREAD

225g (8oz/2 sticks) unsalted butter

100g (3½oz/½ cup) caster (superfine) sugar

100g (3½oz/⅓ cup + 2 tablespoons) light brown sugar

2 large egg yolks

250g (9oz/2 cups) plain white flour

100g (3½oz/¼ cup + 3 tablespoons) plain wholemeal flour

½ teaspoon baking powder

½ teaspoon ground cinnamon

¼ teaspoon fine sea salt

FOR THE APRICOT FILLING

300g (10½oz) stoned apricots (stoned weight), quartered

1 tablespoon ground arrowroot or cornflour (cornstarch)

50g (1¾oz/¼ cup) caster (superfine) sugar

finely grated zest of 1 lemon

1 teaspoon vanilla bean paste

Preheat the oven to 180°C (350°F), Gas Mark 4. Lightly grease the tin and line with a piece of parchment paper, so the excess goes up all the sides of the tin.

For the shortbread, brown the butter in a small saucepan over a medium heat, stirring frequently. The butter will melt, then sizzle and splatter and then it will start to foam. As it foams, you'll see little golden brown flecks start to appear. Before these flecks burn, remove the pan from the heat, pour the butter into a heatproof bowl and refrigerate, stirring occasionally, until the butter is firm but spreadable.

Place the browned butter and both sugars into a large bowl and, using an electric mixer, beat for 2–3 minutes or until light and creamy. Add the egg yolks and mix briefly to combine. In a separate bowl, mix together all the dry ingredients, then add to the butter mixture and mix just until the dough starts to form a uniform mass. Tip about two-thirds of the mixture into the lined tin (reserve the remainder) and press into an even layer using your hands. Dock the shortbread base all over with a fork and then bake for 15–20 minutes, or until just lightly browned. Remove from the oven and set aside.

Meanwhile, for the filling, place the apricots into a medium-sized saucepan. Mix the arrowroot or cornflour, sugar, lemon zest and vanilla together in a bowl, then add this mixture to the pan, stirring to combine. Cook over a medium heat or until the sugar and arrowroot/cornflour have dissolved and the mixture has come to a simmer. The fruit should have lost a little texture but not be mushy. Set aside to cool for 5 minutes.

Spread the fruit mixture evenly over the shortbread base, then crumble over the reserved shortbread mixture in an even layer. Bake for 25–30 minutes, or until the crumble is golden brown.

Leave the crumble bars to cool completely in the tin before carefully removing (using the parchment to help) and cutting into squares.

Store in a sealed container for 2–3 days.

ROASTED WHITE CHOCOLATE OATMEAL RAISIN COOKIE BARS

SERVES 16

I think it is fair to say that chocolate can make almost anything better, and while oatmeal raisin cookies don't really need improving, in this recipe, chocolate turns them into something very, very special. Roasted white chocolate has all the flavours of white chocolate but it's caramelized to make something that tastes almost like dulce de leche.

FOR THE CARAMELIZED WHITE CHOCOLATE GANACHE

370g (13oz) white chocolate, roughly chopped

150ml (5fl oz/½ cup + 2 tablespoons) double (heavy) cream

1½ teaspoons flaked sea salt

FOR THE OATMEAL RAISIN BARS

120g (4¼oz/8½ tablespoons) unsalted butter, plus extra for greasing

125g (4½oz/1 cup) plain (all-purpose) flour

160g (5¾oz/2 cups) rolled oats

½ teaspoon flaked sea salt

3 tablespoons golden syrup or clear honey

150g (5½oz/⅔ cup) light brown sugar

3 tablespoons milk powder

¾ teaspoon bicarbonate of soda (baking soda)

145g (5¼oz/1⅛ cups) raisins, soaked in boiling water, drained

Preheat the oven to 120°C (250°F), Gas Mark ½.

Add the white chocolate for the ganache to the baking tin in a single layer and bake for about 60–90 minutes, stirring vigorously every 15 minutes, until melted and a rich, golden colour. When you take out the chocolate to stir it may look coarse and grainy, ensure you stir it until smooth and melted before returning to the oven. Once it's ready, scrape into a heatproof bowl and set aside.

Increase the oven temperature to 180°C (350°F), Gas Mark 4. Wash and dry the baking tin, grease it, then line with a strip of parchment paper that overhangs the two long sides of the tin. Secure the paper in place with two metal clips.

Place the flour, oats and salt into a large, heatproof bowl and mix together. Place the butter, syrup or honey, sugar and milk powder into a medium-sized saucepan and cook over a low-medium heat until melted and combined. Remove from the heat and whisk in the bicarbonate of soda and 1 tablespoon water, then pour this and the raisins over the oat mixture and stir to coat. While still warm, tip into the prepared tin and press into an even layer.

Bake for 25–30 minutes, or until golden all over and just a little darker around the edges. Leave to cool in the tin for 15 minutes before adding the ganache.

To finish the ganache, pour the cream into the bowl with the roasted chocolate, then place over a pan of simmering water (ensuring the bottom of the bowl doesn't touch the water) and cook, stirring occasionally, until the ganache is smooth and combined. Pour over the base and spread into an even layer, then pop the tin in the refrigerator until set, about 1 hour. Just before the ganache is set, sprinkle with the salt.

Remove from the refrigerator and cut into small bars to serve. Store in a sealed container for 3–4 days.

NOTE When choosing your white chocolate for roasting, use one with at least 30% cocoa butter.

PASTRIES, PIES & TARTS

BLUEBERRY AND STONE-FRUIT GALETTE

SERVES 8–10

Galettes are pies for those who aren't concerned with crimping, cannot be bothered to blind bake or do anything that might be viewed as technical or tricky. Galettes revel in their relative ease and rustic nature, once you learn to make them you'll be knocking them up without thinking, filling them with whatever fruit is in season and making the recipe your own. This is my current favourite, with a pecan-infused pastry generously filled with blueberries and peaches and served, of course, with plenty of vanilla ice cream.

FOR THE GALETTE PASTRY

185g (6½oz/1½ cups) plain (all-purpose) flour, plus extra for dusting

85g (3oz/¾ cup) pecans

1 tablespoon caster (superfine) sugar

½ teaspoon fine sea salt

170g (6oz/1½ sticks) unsalted butter, diced and chilled

4–6 tablespoons ice-cold water

1 large egg, beaten

demerara sugar, for sprinkling

FOR THE FILLING

450g (1lb/3 cups) fresh blueberries

3 peaches or nectarines, stoned and cut into slices

finely grated zest of 1 lemon

1 tablespoon lemon juice

50g (1¾oz/¼ cup) caster (superfine) sugar

2 tablespoons ground arrowroot or cornflour (cornstarch)

pinch of fine sea salt

¼ teaspoon ground cinnamon

100g (3½oz/1 cup) ground almonds

30g (1oz/2 tablespoons) unsalted butter

vanilla ice cream, to serve

For the pastry, place the flour, pecans, sugar and salt into the bowl of a food processor and pulse until the nuts are ground to a coarse meal texture. Add the diced butter and pulse a few times until the butter forms pieces about the size of peas. Add 4 tablespoons of the ice-cold water and pulse a couple of times to combine. To check if it's ready, squeeze a small amount, if it forms a ball of dough the pastry is ready, if not add the remaining 2 tablespoons of the water. Tip the pastry out on to a lightly floured work surface and form into a ball of dough, then press into a flat rectangle, wrap in clingfilm and refrigerate for at least an hour before using.

Preheat the oven to 190°C (375°F), Gas Mark 5.

To make the filling, add the fruit to a large bowl with the lemon zest and juice, tossing together. In a small bowl, mix together the sugar, arrowroot (or cornflour), salt and cinnamon, then add to the fruit mixture, stirring to coat evenly. Set aside.

Roll out the pastry on a sheet of parchment paper into a large rectangle roughly 3mm (⅛in) thick and about 30 x 40cm (12 x 16in), trimming the pastry and parchment paper. If the dough is at all soft at this point. Refrigerate for 15 minutes.

Spread the ground almonds across the centre of the pastry, in a 23 x 33cm (9 x 13in) rectangle. Spoon the fruit filling on to the pastry over the ground almonds. Cut the butter into small pieces and dot over the fruit filling. Fold the excess pastry up and over the fruit filling (the centre of the fruit won't be covered), brush this pastry with the beaten egg and sprinkle liberally with demerara sugar. Use the parchment paper to carefully transfer the galette into the baking tin.

Bake for 45–50 minutes, or until the pastry is golden and the fruit is bubbling. Leave to cool slightly in the tin, before cutting into slices and serving warm, topped with scoops of vanilla ice cream.

This galette is best served warm on the day it's made.

APRICOT AND MASCARPONE POP TARTS

MAKES 8

I have a distinct memory of when Pop Tarts made it to the UK. I desperately wanted to have them for breakfast, they seemed somehow exotic and cool, like everything from the US was to me at that young age. Cut to me finally trying them as an adult and being entirely underwhelmed. The pastry was cardboard-like and the fillings were generally too sweet and artificial-tasting. This recipe is my answer to pop tarts, how I hoped they'd taste. Part toaster strudel, part Pop Tart, they're the ultimate hand pie.

1 batch of flaky pastry (see page 88)

unsalted butter or neutral-tasting oil, for greasing

8 tablespoons mascarpone

8 tablespoons apricot jam

1 teaspoon vanilla bean paste

1 large egg yolk, beaten

3 tablespoons lemon juice

180g (6⅓oz/1½ cups) icing (powdered) sugar

colourful sprinkles, to decorate (optional)

Make the pastry according to the recipe on page 88, dividing the dough into two halves and chilling it for at least an hour before using.

Lightly grease the base of the baking tin and line with a piece of parchment paper.

Take one of the chilled dough halves and roll it out on a lightly floured surface to fit the baking tin, trimming to make a neat rectangle, then carefully place the pastry into the tin. Use a knife to score the pastry into eight equal sections. Spread a tablespoon of mascarpone on to each section of pastry, leaving a clear thin border around the edge. Mix the jam and vanilla together and place a tablespoon of jam on to each section, spreading it over the mascarpone. Brush the exposed pastry borders with beaten egg yolk.

Roll out the remaining piece of pastry just a little bigger than before and then carefully drape it over the first, trying not to disturb the fillings too much. Use your fingers to gently press around the fillings to seal the pastry pieces together. Use a sharp knife to cut between the tarts and then use a fork to create a decorative edge for each pastry and further seal the edges. Poke a steam vent in each tart with a fork and brush with the beaten egg yolk. Chill in the refrigerator for 30 minutes before baking.

Preheat the oven to 190°C (375°F), Gas Mark 5.

Bake the pop tarts for 20–30 minutes, or until the pastry is golden brown. Leave to cool in the tin for five minutes before transferring to a wire rack to cool completely.

Mix together the lemon juice and icing sugar in a bowl until smooth. If the pastries haven't separated fully as they bake, cut with a knife to separate. Spoon a little glaze over each pastry, and if you want the full pop tart experience, add a few colourful sprinkles. Serve warm or cold.

Store in a sealed container for a couple of days, or freeze without the glaze for up to a month.

GRAPEFRUIT MERINGUE PIE

SERVES 10–12

The classic citrus tart filling can be made a few different ways. You can make a custard that is baked in the oven, a stovetop curd or a butter-rich citrus cream. While I have love for each of these methods, more and more I want something a little simpler. This recipe uses the easier pastry cream method. The grapefruit custard is made on the stovetop, using cornflour to thicken the custard, which makes the filling more foolproof.

1 fully baked 23 x 33cm (9 x 13in) tart case (see page 78)

FOR THE CUSTARD FILLING

350g (12oz/1¾ cups) caster (superfine) sugar

50g (1¾oz/6 tablespoons) cornflour (cornstarch)

finely grated zest of 2 ruby grapefruits

finely grated zest of 3 limes

360ml (12½fl oz/1½ cups) ruby grapefruit juice (from 3–4 large grapefruits)

90ml (3¼fl oz/6 tablespoons) lime juice (from about 4 limes)

4 large egg yolks

160ml (5½fl oz/⅔ cup) double (heavy) cream

30g (1oz/2 tablespoons) unsalted butter

FOR THE MERINGUE TOPPING

4 large egg whites

300g (10½oz/1½ cups) caster (superfine) sugar

¼ teaspoon cream of tartar

1 teaspoon vanilla bean paste

¼ teaspoon grapefruit (or other citrus) bitters

To make the custard filling, place the caster sugar and cornflour into a large saucepan and whisk to combine. Add the remaining ingredients, except the butter, and whisk to combine. Cook over a medium-high heat, whisking constantly, until the mixture comes to a simmer, then cook for a further 2 minutes until thick. Remove from the heat, stir through the butter until melted and smooth, then pour the custard into the baked tart case. Press a sheet of clingfilm on to the surface of the custard to prevent a skin from forming. Leave at room temperature for an hour, then transfer to the refrigerator for at least 4 hours.

For the meringue topping, place the egg whites, sugar and cream of tartar into a large, heatproof bowl set over a pan of simmering water (ensuring the bottom of the bowl doesn't touch the water underneath) and whisk until the sugar has dissolved. You can tell when this mixture is ready by rubbing a little between your fingers. If it feels smooth it is ready, if you feel grains of sugar cook for longer. Remove the bowl from the heat and, using an electric mixer, whisk until stiff and glossy. Add the vanilla and bitters and whisk briefly to combine. Scrape the meringue on to the tart and spread over the filling. Using a blowtorch or under a preheated hot grill (broiler), burnish the meringue until toasted.

Kept in the refrigerator, without the meringue, this tart will keep for a couple of days, but my preference is to serve it as close to making as possible to keep the pastry at its crispest.

BERRY ALMOND FRANGIPANE TART

SERVES 12

Frangipane is one of those classic elements that once learned can be used to make all manner of dishes, and it can also be made with all sorts of ground nuts. For this tart, I have kept things simple, making a spin on the classic Bakewell tart using blackberries instead of cherries or raspberries. While I have used blackberries, you can make this dish with all sorts of berries, simply match the berries and jam to make your own version.

FOR THE SWEET PASTRY

300g (10½oz/2 cups + 6 tablespoons) plain (all-purpose) flour

50g (1¾oz/7 tablespoons) icing sugar

¼ teaspoon fine sea salt

185g (6½oz/13 tablespoons) unsalted butter, diced and chilled

1 large egg

FOR THE ALMOND FRANGIPANE

170g (6oz/1½ sticks) unsalted butter, at room temperature

175g (6oz/¾ cup + 1 tablespoon) caster (superfine) sugar

3 large eggs

½ teaspoon almond extract

170g (6oz/1¾ cups) ground almonds

5 tablespoons berry jam

250g (9oz) fresh berries

3 tablespoons flaked almonds

NOTE If you're using this pastry for another recipe and you're not baking it again with a filling, bake for a further 10 minutes at step 5, or until the base is golden.

For the pastry, place the flour, icing sugar and salt in a food processor and pulse briefly together to combine. Add the butter and pulse until the mixture resembles breadcrumbs, then add the egg and pulse until the mixture starts to clump together. At this point, you can either use the dough as a press-in crust or chill it and roll it out. If rolling it, tip the mixture on to the work surface and bring it together as a dough with your hands. Form into a rectangle, wrap in clingfilm and refrigerate for at least an hour before using.

If using as a press-in crust, tip the mixture directly into the baking tin and loosely spread evenly to cover the bottom of the tin. Press up the sides of the tin to create the tart sides, then firmly press the remaining pastry over the base. Dock with a fork and refrigerate for at least an hour before baking. If rolling, roll out between two sheets of parchment paper into a rectangle, roughly 30.5 x 40.5cm (12 x 16in). Transfer to a baking tray and refrigerate for another 30 minutes to firm up. Lightly grease the tin and line the base with parchment paper.

Preheat the oven to 180°C (350°F), Gas Mark 4.

Peel the parchment paper from both sides of the pastry and carefully drape the pastry into the baking tin, gently pressing it into the corners and up the sides. Trim off the top edges then line with a piece of crumpled parchment paper and fill with baking beans or rice. Bake for 25 minutes, then remove the paper and beans/rice and bake for a further 10 minutes or until the base is set. Set aside.

Meanwhile, for the frangipane, beat the butter and caster sugar together in a bowl using an electric mixer until light and fluffy, about 5 minutes, then add the eggs, one at a time, until combined. Beat in the almond extract and ground almonds. Spread the jam over the base of the tart and top evenly with the frangipane. Top with the berries and flaked almonds. Bake for 30–35 minutes or until golden.

Remove from the oven and allow the tart to cool completely in the tin before serving.

Kept covered or in a sealed container, this will keep for 2 days.

PUMPKIN PIE WITH OREO CRUST

SERVES 10–12

This version of pumpkin pie is far from traditional. Firstly, it uses an Oreo cookie base, and secondly, the custard is made without eggs. These two changes make the classic Thanksgiving pie easier than normal but also makes it vegan (see Note). It can also be a no-bake pie. Simply chill the base instead of baking it, and cook the filling on the stovetop, pouring the mixture into a large saucepan and whisking while cooking until it bubbles and thickens. Pour into the chilled pie crust and refrigerate for 4 hours until set.

neutral-tasting oil, for greasing

FOR THE OREO CRUST

36 chocolate sandwich cookies

60g (2½oz/4 tablespoons) coconut oil, melted and cooled

FOR THE PUMPKIN CUSTARD FILLING

425g (15oz) can pumpkin purée (not pumpkin pie filling)

240ml (8½fl oz/1 cup) unsweetened almond or light coconut milk

1 teaspoon ground cinnamon

½ teaspoon ground ginger

¼ teaspoon freshly grated nutmeg

pinch of ground cardamom

¼ teaspoon fine sea salt

40g (1½oz/⅓ cup) cornflour (cornstarch)

180ml (6¼fl oz/¾ cup) maple syrup

FOR THE COCONUT WHIPPED CREAM

400ml (14fl oz) can coconut milk, chilled in the refrigerator overnight

2 tablespoons maple syrup

1 teaspoon vanilla bean paste

Preheat the oven to 190°C (375°F), Gas Mark 5. Lightly grease the baking tin and line the base with a piece of parchment paper.

For the crust, place the cookies into a food processor and pulse until finely ground. Pour in the coconut oil and pulse until evenly combined. If you don't have a food processor, you can crush the cookies to crumbs in a sealed ziplock bag, bashing them with a rolling pin, then tip the crumbs into a large bowl and mix through the coconut oil. Tip the crust mixture into the prepared tin and firmly press into an even layer, pressing a little up the sides as well.

Bake for 10 minutes, then remove from the oven and set aside.

Reduce the oven temperature to 180°C (350°F), Gas Mark 4.

For the filling, place all the ingredients into a large bowl and whisk together until smooth. Pour the filling into the Oreo crust and spread into an even layer.

Bake for 40–45 minutes, or until the custard is set around the edges and with just a little wobble in the middle. Leave to cool completely in the tin before serving.

For the coconut whipped cream, remove the coconut milk from the refrigerator and open the can. Carefully scoop the solid coconut cream from the top of the can into a large bowl, leaving behind the clear liquid (discard this). Whisk the coconut cream using an electric mixer until it holds soft peaks. Gently stir through the maple syrup and vanilla. You can either spread this over the entire pie or cut the pie into squares and dollop the cream on top when serving.

This pie is best served on the day it's made.

NOTE Oreo brand cookies were, for years, thought to be vegan, but recently it was confirmed that they can't be classified as vegan due to potential cross-contamination. Many other brands of this style of chocolate sandwich cookies are, however, vegan.

GIANT PORTUGUESE CUSTARD TART

SERVES 8–10

I am an advocate for pasteis de nata and I will tell anyone who'll listen that Portuguese custard tarts are one of the best baked goods around. If they're still listening, I'll also tell them which bakery in Lisbon serves the best (it's Manteigaria, if you're asking). This recipe is my homage to these delightful Portuguese tarts. Pasteis de nata are notoriously hard to replicate at home as domestic ovens don't generally get hot enough. Thankfully, I have come up with a workaround that replicates a bakery-style rack oven at home in a regular domestic oven.

unsalted butter or neutral-tasting oil, for greasing

320g (1¼oz) sheet ready-rolled all-butter puff pastry

2 large egg yolks, beaten, for brushing

icing (powdered) sugar and ground cinnamon, for dusting

FOR THE CUSTARD FILLING

250g (9oz/1½ cups) caster (superfine) sugar

1 cinnamon stick, broken in half

4 strips orange zest

360ml (12½fl oz/1½ cups) double (heavy) cream

300ml (10fl oz/1¼ cups) whole milk

1 teaspoon vanilla bean paste

3 large eggs, plus 3 large egg yolks

50g (1¾oz/6 tablespoons) cornflour (cornstarch)

For the custard filling, place 240ml (8½fl oz/1 cup) water, the sugar, cinnamon and orange zest into a saucepan and bring to a simmer over a medium heat, cooking for a couple of minutes until the sugar has fully dissolved. Remove from the heat, cover and set aside.

Lightly grease the baking tin and line the base with parchment paper. Arrange the shelves of the oven so two are close together, leaving about a 13cm (5in) gap between them. On both shelves, place a pizza stone or baking steel, if you have one, otherwise use two stacked baking trays per shelf. You can make this without the pizza stones/baking steels/baking trays, but the effect won't be quite as close to the real deal.

Preheat the oven to 190°C (375°F), Gas Mark 5 30 minutes before the tart is ready to bake.

Unroll the puff pastry and roll out into a rectangle that is roughly 3mm (⅛in) thick. Trim the pastry into a neat 28 x 38cm (11 x 15in) rectangle and drape into the prepared baking tin. Freeze for about 10 minutes or until the pastry is solid. Line the pastry case with a crumpled piece of parchment paper and fill with baking beans or rice.

Transfer to the rack you have assembled in the oven and bake for 20 minutes, then remove the beans/rice and parchment paper and bake for a further 10 minutes until lightly browned. Brush the inside with the beaten egg yolks, then bake for a further 2 minutes, or until the yolks are set. Remove from the oven and set aside. Increase the oven temperature to 240°C (475°F), Gas Mark 9, or as hot as your oven will go.

To finish the custard filling, tip the cream, milk and vanilla into a large saucepan and bring to a simmer. Place the eggs, egg yolks and cornflour in a heatproof bowl and whisk together until smooth. Pour the hot cream mixture over the eggs, whisking to combine, then pour the cream mixture back into the pan.

CONTINUED OVERLEAF

Pour the sugar syrup into the pan, pouring it through a sieve to remove the cinnamon and orange. Place the pan over a medium heat and cook, whisking constantly, until the mixture comes to the boil and thickens. Immediately pour into the blind-baked tart case and spread evenly.

Bake on the rack in the oven for about 20 minutes, or until the custard is burnished. As the tart is larger than a traditional custard tart, it won't brown all the way to the middle before the egg overcooks, so take it out while the centre of the tart is still yellow. Leave to cool completely in the tin before serving.

To serve, dust with a little icing sugar and ground cinnamon, cut into portions and serve alongside a strong coffee.

This tart is best served on the day it is made and within a few hours of baking.

VANILLA SLICES

MAKES 12

When my twin brother and I were little, and if we were giving our parents a rare moment of peace and quiet, we used to get a little treat from the bakery near our house. My choice was always a Yorkshire curd tart or an egg custard tart, but my brother would usually choose a classic vanilla slice – a thick layer of bright yellow custard sandwiched between two layers of puff pastry. It's so simple, so comforting, and it's such a wonderfully easy recipe. My version sticks closely to the traditional recipe, except I forgo the layer of icing that is often found on top, it's just added sweetness with no extra flavour so I prefer them as is. They are best made a day in advance to allow the custard to fully set in the refrigerator overnight.

2 x 320g (11¼oz) sheets of ready-rolled all-butter puff pastry

750ml (1⅓ pints/3 cups + 2 tablespoons) whole milk

320ml (10½fl oz/1⅓ cups) double (heavy) cream

seeds scraped from 1 vanilla pod or 2 teaspoons vanilla bean paste

250g (9oz/1¼ cups) caster (superfine) sugar

75g (2¾oz/9 tablespoons) custard powder (see Note overleaf)

3 large eggs

¼ teaspoon fine sea salt

75g (2¾oz/⅔ stick) unsalted butter, diced

icing sugar, for dusting

Preheat the oven to 190°C (375°F), Gas Mark 5. Line the base of the baking tin with parchment paper.

Unroll the first puff pastry sheet and trim so it fits neatly inside your prepared tin. Place it into the tin and dock with a fork, then cover with a sheet of parchment paper. Weigh the puff pastry down with a second baking tin, ideally one which nests neatly inside the first one, or weigh it down with some metal cutlery.

Bake for 20 minutes, then remove the weight and top sheet of paper and bake for a further 5–10 minutes, or until golden brown. Leave to cool slightly in the tin, then transfer to a wire rack to cool completely. Repeat with the second sheet of puff pastry using the same lined baking tin.

Once both sheets of baked pastry are cold, line the base and sides of the empty baking tin with a large sheet of foil so the excess goes up the sides and lay the first sheet of puff pastry inside the tin.

For the custard, place the milk and cream into a large saucepan with the vanilla seeds, along with the empty vanilla pod, too. Bring the milk mixture to a simmer, then remove from the heat, cover and set aside for an hour or so to infuse. If using vanilla bean paste, skip this infusion step.

In a large, heatproof bowl, whisk together the caster sugar and custard powder, then add the eggs and salt and whisk until smooth and lump-free. Bring the milk mixture back to a simmer, then pour it over the egg mixture, whisking to prevent curdling. Remove the vanilla pod or add the vanilla bean paste at this point, then pour the custard back into the pan and cook over a medium heat, whisking constantly, until the custard thickens and is bubbling.

CONTINUED OVERLEAF

NOTE If you live in a country where custard powder (a product that is mainly cornflour and flavouring) isn't readily available, you can use an equal amount of cornflour instead. Your custard won't have the classic yellow hue as custard powder contains a little colouring.

Remove from the heat and stir in the butter until it has fully melted into the custard. Immediately pour the custard into the baking tin over the first sheet of puff pastry and spread evenly. Place the second sheet of pastry on top, pressing gently to secure in place.

Wrap the tin in clingfilm and refrigerate for at least 4 hours to allow the custard to fully set. Once chilled and set, use the foil to carefully lift the mixture from the tin. Dust with icing sugar, then use a sharp knife to cut it into slices.

Stored in a sealed container in the refrigerator these will keep for a couple of days, but they are best served as close to making as possible.

SLAB ECCLES CAKE

SERVES 12

For my non-British friends, while this might have the word cake in its title, it's most definitely made of pastry. This is a classic British bake and a big favourite in my family. Traditionally, it is a small round of flaky pastry filled with a sweet, spiced currant mixture. It is named after Eccles, the small town in Lancashire it hails from. You can make this with ready-made puff pastry, but I would encourage you to try my homemade flaky pastry as it makes it so much better.

FOR THE FLAKY PASTRY

350g (12oz/2¾ cups) plain (all-purpose) flour, plus extra for dusting

1 teaspoon fine sea salt

300g (10½oz/2⅔ sticks) unsalted butter, diced

10–12 tablespoons ice-cold water

1 large egg white, lightly beaten

granulated sugar, for sprinkling

FOR THE ECCLES CAKE FILLING

370g (13oz) currants

165g (5¾oz/¾ cup) dark brown sugar

1¼ teaspoons freshly grated nutmeg

1½ teaspoons ground allspice

¾ teaspoon ground cinnamon

75g (2¾oz/⅔ stick) unsalted butter, melted

3 tablespoons brandy (Armagnac is my favourite)

finely grated zest of 1 large orange

large pinch of flaked sea salt

NOTE If you have time, prepare the filling the day before to let it mature a little in the refrigerator, but if not, make it after the pastry and chill it.

For the pastry, mix the flour and salt in a large bowl. Add the diced butter and toss in the flour, then use your fingertips to press the pieces of butter into flat flakes. Chill in the refrigerator for 15 minutes to firm up the butter. Drizzle in the water, a little at a time, stirring in with a round-bladed knife. When the mixture is starting to hold together, use your hands to bring briefly together into a uniform dough. Shape into a rectangle, wrap in clingfilm and refrigerate for 30 minutes.

Roll out the chilled dough on a lightly floured surface into a 40 x 20cm (16 x 8in) rectangle. Fold the dough into thirds like a business letter, wrap in clingfilm, then refrigerate for a further 30 minutes. With the open seams of the dough facing you, roll out again into a 40 x 20cm (16 x 8in) rectangle, then fold as before. Cut the dough in half, wrap in clingfilm and chill for a final 30 minutes.

To make the filling, mix the currants, sugar and spices together in a bowl. Add the melted butter, brandy, orange zest and salt and stir together until evenly combined. Refrigerate while the pastry chills.

Preheat the oven to 200°C (400°F), Gas Mark 6. Line the base of the baking tin with parchment paper.

Roll out one piece of pastry on a lightly floured surface into a 23 x 33cm (9 x 13in) rectangle. Line the prepared tin with this sheet, then spread over the filling, leaving a 1–2cm (½–¾in) border around the outside. Roll out the second piece of pastry just a little bigger than before and place on top of the filling, using a fork to seal the two pieces of pastry together. Brush the pastry with the egg white and sprinkle liberally with granulated sugar, then cut a few vent holes in the top.

Bake for 30–35 minutes, or until deep golden brown. Leave to cool to room temperature in the tin before serving.

While I love this served as it is, a wedge of Cheddar also pairs wonderfully. It is best served on the day it's made, still a little warm, but will keep in a sealed container for a few days.

SLAB CHERRY PIE

SERVES 12–15

There is something cruel when it comes to my favourite pie season, summer. Fruit is plentiful, but the heat of summer makes it the trickiest time to make pastry! Thankfully, the rustic nature of a homemade pie is joyous.

Pastry cut-outs are a lot easier than a lattice crust and are equally as pretty. I use a mix of fresh sweet cherries and frozen sour cherries, roughly half and half, because sour cherries can be hard to come by. If you want to use only sour cherries, increase the sugar a little to compensate for the tartness.

FOR THE FLAKY PIE DOUGH

400g (14oz/3 cups + 3 tablespoons) plain (all-purpose) flour, plus extra for dusting

4 tablespoons caster (superfine) sugar

1½ teaspoons fine sea salt

340g (11¾oz/3 sticks) unsalted butter, diced and chilled

7–8 tablespoons ice-cold water

3 tablespoons vodka

beaten egg, to glaze

demerara sugar, for sprinkling

FOR THE CHERRY FILLING

1kg (1lb 4oz) cherries, fresh or frozen, pitted (see intro)

1 tablespoon lemon juice

2 teaspoons almond extract (optional)

175g (6oz/¾ cup + ⅛ cup) caster (superfine) sugar

3 tablespoons ground arrowroot (or cornflour)

vanilla ice cream, to serve

NOTE To avoid the dreaded soggy bottom, bake on top of something solid and preheated; a pizza stone, baking steel or large baking sheet work well.

Make the pastry with the listed ingredients according to the method on page 92.

Cut off about two-thirds of the chilled dough (pop the remainder back into the refrigerator), then roll out on a lightly floured surface into a rectangle, roughly 3mm (⅛in) thick. Trim the dough to 30.5 x 40.5cm (12 x 16in) and use it to line the tin, gently pressing it into the corners and up the sides. Trim off the top edges evenly with a knife, then refrigerate while you make the filling.

Meanwhile, preheat the oven to 220°C (425°F), Gas Mark 7.

For the filling, place the cherries into a large bowl and toss together with the lemon juice and almond extract (if using). In a small bowl, whisk together the sugar and arrowroot, then sprinkle this over the cherries and mix together.

Roll out the remaining pastry on a lightly floured surface to about 3mm (⅛in) thick. Use small, round, fluted cookie cutters in a variety of sizes to cut out as many rounds of pastry as possible.

Pour the cherry mixture into the prepared pastry case, then top randomly with the pastry cut-outs and crimp the edges of the pie. Brush the pastry with a little beaten egg and sprinkle liberally with demerara sugar.

Bake for 15 minutes, then reduce the temperature to 180°C (350°F), Gas Mark 4 and bake for a further 35–45 minutes, or until the pastry is golden brown and the filling is bubbling. If the pastry starts to brown before the filling bubbles, lightly tent the pie with foil.

Leave to cool in the tin. Serve warm or cold, either on its own or with a scoop of vanilla ice cream.

Kept covered, this pie will keep for about 2–3 days.

PASTRIES, PIES & TARTS

WHISKEY AND RYE PEACH PIE

SERVES 10–12

Peach pie is an absolute classic, and while the title of this recipe might make it seem like I have messed around with the flavours, the truth is everything has been included to enhance the taste of the peaches. For the filling, I like to let the fruit and sugar mingle together for a while to draw out the juices. These are then reduced with a little lemon juice for brightness. Thickening the juices in this manner is a great tip when making fruit pies, as it concentrates the flavour and reduces the amount of liquid produced, which prevents a soggy bottom crust.

FOR THE RYE FLOUR PASTRY

250g (9oz/2 cups) plain (all-purpose) flour, plus extra for dusting

150g (5½oz/1½ cups) wholemeal rye flour

4 tablespoons caster (superfine) sugar

1½ teaspoons fine sea salt

340g (11¾oz/3 sticks) unsalted butter, diced and chilled

about 10 tablespoons ice-cold water

1 large egg, beaten

demerara sugar, for sprinkling

FOR THE PEACH FILLING

6 large peaches, about 1.25kg (2lb 12oz), peeled and stoned

125g (4½oz/½ cup + ⅛ cup) caster (superfine) sugar

juice of ½ lemon

60ml (2¼fl oz/¼ cup) whiskey or bourbon

couple of drops of almond extract (optional)

¼ teaspoon ground cinnamon

¼ teaspoon ground ginger

pinch of fine sea salt

30g (1oz/¼ cup) ground arrowroot or cornflour (cornstarch)

20g (¾oz/1½ tablespoons) unsalted butter, diced

To make the pastry, place both flours, the sugar and salt into a large bowl and mix together. Rub in about a quarter of the butter until it resembles fine breadcrumbs. Add the remaining butter, toss in the flour mixture, then press the butter into flat flakes. Pop the bowl into the freezer for 15 minutes, then drizzle in the ice-cold water, a few tablespoons at a time, stirring with a round-bladed knife. As the dough starts to come together, squeeze a small amount together, if it holds its shape it's ready, if it crumbles, add a little more water. Tip the mixture out on to the work surface and bring together as a ball of dough (it shouldn't be sticky). Press into a flat rectangle, wrap in clingfilm and refrigerate for 20 minutes.

Roll out the dough on a lightly floured work surface to a rectangle roughly 20 x 40cm (8 x 16in). Roll the dough up into a fat sausage and cut in half. Form each piece of dough into a flat rectangle, wrap in clingfilm and refrigerate for at least an hour before using.

For the filling, slice the peaches into a large bowl and toss together with the sugar. Set aside for an hour.

Pour the fruit into a large, fine mesh sieve set over a large saucepan and leave for a few minutes to drain. Tip the fruit back into the bowl, then add the lemon juice and whiskey or bourbon to the pan. Cook over a medium-high heat until the liquid has reduced by half. Remove from the heat, stir in the almond extract (if using) and pour over the sliced peaches. Add the spices, salt and arrowroot and toss to mix. Set aside.

To assemble the pie, take one piece of pastry and roll it out on a lightly floured work surface into a rectangle about 30.5 x 40.5cm (12 x 16in). Transfer to the baking tin and trim so the sides of the pie are level, then refrigerate. Roll out the second piece of pastry into a rectangle about 25 x 35cm (10 x 14in), transfer to a sheet of parchment paper, then use a few different-sized round cookie cutters to cut out several holes across the pastry (leaving the outer 2.5cm/1in clear). Chill until the pastry is firm enough to lift but not too stiff.

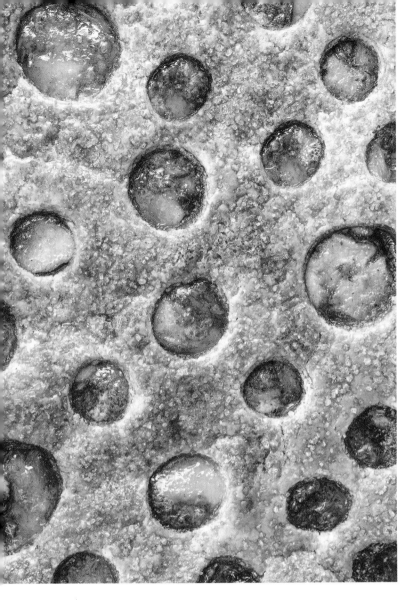

Preheat the oven to 190°C (375°F), Gas Mark 5.

Pour the peach filling into the chilled base, dotting over the pieces of butter. Carefully place the lid of pastry on the top of the pie, using a fork to seal the two pieces together. Brush the pie with beaten egg and sprinkle liberally with demerara sugar.

Bake for 50–60 minutes, or until the pastry is golden and the filling is bubbling. With a pie this size, ensure the filling is bubbling in the middle so it is fully set.

Leave to cool before serving. The pie can be served warm or at room temperature.

This pie is best served on the day it's made, but will keep for 2–3 days if covered.

NOTE If you want to ensure the pastry on the base of the pie is fully baked, I like to bake pies like this on a pizza stone or baking steel. You can also preheat a baking tray in the oven, then bake the pie on this, which will help to brown the bottom crust as well.

PEANUT BUTTER CHOCOLATE TART

SERVES 12–14

While I love pastry, sometimes I don't have the patience or time to make it, so in those times, I turn to cookie crusts – tart cases made with a mixture of cookie crumbs and butter. They're incredibly quick and simple to throw together, but they do have one down side: they're not the easiest to remove from the tin, so they're best served in the tin. My way around this is to mix in an egg white, which acts like glue, holding all of the ingredients together. For this tart, I have stuck with the flavours of two of my favourite candy aisle treats, peanut butter cups and Oreos, a candy and cookie which I think are pretty much perfect.

FOR THE OREO CRUST

36 Oreo cookies

60g (2¼oz/4 tablespoons) unsalted butter, melted and cooled

1 large egg white

¼ teaspoon flaked sea salt

FOR THE PEANUT BUTTER FILLING

315g (11oz/1½ cups) smooth peanut butter

45g (1¾oz/3 tablespoons) unsalted butter, at room temperature

60g (2½oz/½ cup) icing (powdered) sugar

1 teaspoon vanilla bean paste

360ml (12½fl oz/1½ cups) double (heavy) cream

FOR THE CHOCOLATE TOPPING

200g (7oz) dark chocolate (60–70% cocoa solids), finely chopped

60ml (2¼fl oz/¼ cup) double (heavy) cream

15g (½oz/1 tablespoon) unsalted butter

flaked sea salt, for sprinkling

Preheat the oven to 180°C (350°F), Gas Mark 4 and line the baking tin with a large piece of parchment paper that covers all the sides of the tin.

For the crust, place the Oreos into a food processor and process to fine crumbs. Pour in the melted butter, egg white and salt, and process until evenly mixed. Tip the crumb mixture into the prepared tin and press evenly across the base and a little up the sides of the tin. Refrigerate for 20 minutes.

Bake the crust for 12–15 minutes, or until set. If the crust loses definition as it bakes, use a glass to gently press back into shape. You can serve the tart in the baking tin, if you prefer, but the benefit of lining the tin and making the crust with egg white means that you can lift the baked tart from the tin (once thoroughly chilled) and assemble and serve it on a platter.

For the filling, beat the peanut butter, butter, icing sugar and vanilla together in a bowl until smooth. Pour in a quarter of the cream and mix until combined, then repeat with a further quarter of the cream. In a separate bowl, whip the remaining cream until it holds soft peaks, then carefully fold this into the peanut butter mixture, in two separate additions. Spread the filling into the tart crust in an even layer and refrigerate while you make the topping.

Place the chocolate and cream into a heatproof bowl set over a pan of simmering water (ensuring the bottom of the bowl doesn't touch the water underneath) and heat, stirring occasionally, until fully melted. Remove the bowl from the heat and add the butter, stirring until combined. Allow to cool for 5 minutes, then pour over the filling and spread into an even layer.

Return the tart to the refrigerator for 20–30 minutes, or until the chocolate topping has set. Sprinkle with a little flaked sea salt and cut into thin slices to serve.

This tart is best served on the day it's made.

PISTACHIO CRÈME BRÛLÉE TART WITH HONEY-ROASTED APRICOTS

SERVES 12

This is a dish for a very special occasion. It takes a little bit of preparation but nothing too difficult and it is a sure-fire winner that will impress anyone you serve it to. One of the main ingredients is pistachio paste, basically pistachios puréed until smooth like peanut butter. If you can buy it, it will be incredibly smooth, but if you can't find it, you can make your own by blending blanched and peeled pistachios in a food processor with a pinch of salt until smooth. You'll need to make the custard a day in advance, as it needs to chill overnight.

butter or neutral-tasting oil, for greasing

1 x fully baked 23 x 33cm (9 x 13in) tart case (see page 78)

FOR THE PISTACHIO CRÈME BRÛLÉE CUSTARD

750ml (1⅓ pints/3 cups + 2 tablespoons) double (heavy) cream

1 large egg

8 large egg yolks

100g (3½oz/½ cup) caster (superfine) sugar, plus extra for sprinkling

100g (3½oz/⅓ cup + 1 tablespoon) pistachio paste

2 teaspoons vanilla bean paste

FOR THE HONEY-ROASTED APRICOTS

4 fresh apricots, stoned and sliced

½ teaspoon vanilla bean paste

2 tablespoons clear honey

2 tablespoons lemon juice

For the pistachio custard, pour the cream into a medium-sized saucepan and bring to a simmer. Meanwhile, whisk together the remaining custard ingredients in a large, heatproof bowl until smooth.

Pour the hot cream over the egg mixture, whisking to prevent curdling. Place the bowl of custard over a pan of simmering water (ensuring the bottom of the bowl doesn't touch the water underneath) and then cook, stirring constantly with a spatula, for 10–15 minutes, or until the custard has thickened and coats the back of a wooden spoon (if you want to check the temperature, the custard should reach 75–80°C/170–175°F). Remove the bowl from the heat and press a sheet of clingfilm on to the surface of the custard, then cool and refrigerate overnight.

Preheat the oven to 180°C (350°F), Gas Mark 4.

For the roasted apricots, place the apricot slices into the tin, then drizzle over the vanilla, honey and lemon juice and gently toss together. Bake for 15–20 minutes or until the fruit is softened. Set aside until cool.

To assemble, fill the baked tart case with the roasted apricot slices and then spread the pistachio custard evenly over the top. Sprinkle the tart with a thin layer of sugar, then use a chef's blowtorch to melt and caramelize the sugar. The heat of the blowtorch can soften the custard a little, so I prefer to then place the tart in the refrigerator for an hour or two before serving so it can firm up again. Don't leave the tart in the refrigerator much longer as the sugar will start to weep and soften. Cut into slices and serve.

Once assembled, this tart is best served on the day it's made.

NOTE Pistachio paste should have no added sugar (this would make it a praline paste), but if yours does then reduce the sugar accordingly.

CHOCOLATE CREAM PIE

SERVES 10–12

Sometimes you just want chocolate. With no added flavours or fancy pairings. Just pure chocolate. In these moments, I implore you to make this tart filled with a silky-smooth, rich chocolate custard, topped with a brown sugar whipped cream and a snowstorm of chocolate shavings.

1 fully baked 23 x 33cm (9 x 13in) tart case (see page 78)

FOR THE FILLING

5 tablespoons cornflour (cornstarch)

4 tablespoons cocoa powder

1 teaspoon flaked sea salt

250g (9oz/1¼ cups) caster (superfine) sugar

750ml (25fl oz/3 cups + 3 tablespoons) whole milk

6 large egg yolks

225g (8oz) dark chocolate (65–70% cocoa solids), roughly chopped

30g (1oz/2 tablespoons) unsalted butter, diced

FOR THE TOPPING

600ml (20fl oz/2½ cups) double (heavy) cream

2 tablespoons light brown sugar

1 teaspoon vanilla bean paste

TO DECORATE

100g (3½oz) dark chocolate (65–70% cocoa solids), melted

To make the filling, place the cornflour, cocoa, salt and sugar into a large, heatproof bowl and whisk to combine. Add about 120ml (4fl oz/½ cup) of the milk and the egg yolks and whisk until smooth. Pour the remaining milk into a large saucepan and bring to a simmer. Pour the hot milk over the cocoa mixture, whisking to combine. Pour the custard mixture back into the saucepan and cook over a medium-high heat, whisking constantly, until bubbling, then cook for a further 2 minutes to cook out the starch. You can either assemble this in the tin or carefully remove the baked pastry case from the tin before filling.

Remove from the heat and stir in the chocolate and butter until melted and smooth. Pour the custard into the baked pastry case and spread evenly. Cover with clingfilm and leave at room temperature for an hour, then transfer to the refrigerator for at least 4 hours before serving.

For the topping, place the cream, sugar and vanilla into a large bowl and whisk together just until the mixture holds soft peaks. Scrape the cream on to the tart and spread evenly over the custard.

Pour the melted chocolate over the back of a baking tray (or the back of your empty baking tin) and spread into a thin, even layer. Place the tray in the freezer for a few minutes or just until the chocolate loses its gloss but is not set hard. Use a bench scraper or metal spatula to scrape the chocolate into curls and shards. If the chocolate becomes too soft, return the tray to the freezer.

Scatter the chocolate over the tart, cut into slices and serve.

Store in a sealed container in the refrigerator for a couple of days, but I prefer to serve it as close to making as possible to keep the pastry at its crispest.

WHOLE LEMON BUTTERMILK CHESS PIE

SERVES 12

Chess Pie is an American classic, a true southern favourite. It's not really known where the 'chess' moniker comes from, but my favourite of the many stories attributes the name to the southern accent. The cook that supposedly invented the dish called it 'just pie' and if you do your best southern belle impression, you can almost understand and hear the name. For my version, I've taken that chess pie idea and mashed it together with another favourite, whole lemon tart. It's unusual in that instead of just the zest and juice, the whole lemon is used to make the tart, creating a perfect, sharp summer dish.

butter, for greasing

1 batch of Sweet Pastry (see page 78)

FOR THE FILLING

2 unwaxed lemons

250g (9oz/1¼ cups) caster (superfine) sugar

5 large eggs

360ml (12½fl oz/1½ cups) buttermilk

50g (1¾oz/3½ tablespoons) unsalted butter, melted and cooled

1 teaspoon vanilla extract

2 tablespoons plain (all-purpose) flour

2 tablespoons coarse cornmeal

¼ teaspoon fine sea salt

icing (powdered) sugar, for dusting

Preheat the oven to 190°C (375°F), Gas Mark 5. Lightly grease the baking tin and line the base with a piece of parchment paper.

Roll out the pastry and line the prepared tin as described on page 78. Line the pastry case with a crumpled piece of parchment paper and fill with baking beans or rice, then blind-bake for 25 minutes. Remove the parchment paper and beans and bake for a further 10 minutes, or until the base of the pastry is starting to brown. Remove from the oven and set aside.

Reduce the heat to 180°C (350°F), Gas Mark 4.

For the filling, slice the lemons and remove the seeds. If the pith is particularly thick (over 5mm/¼in), the recipe may be a little too bitter and if that's not desired, then you can cut away some of the pith. Otherwise, place the sliced lemons and sugar into the bowl of a food processor and process for 1–2 minutes until smooth. Add the eggs, buttermilk, melted butter and vanilla and pulse for 30 seconds until combined. Add the flour, cornmeal and salt and pulse for 10–20 seconds to combine.

Pour the filling evenly into the prepared pastry case and bake for about 25 minutes, or until the filling is just set.

Set aside to cool completely in the tin before dusting with icing sugar to serve. If you want to replicate the design I've used, use two straight-edged pieces of card, placed on top of the tart, to create a template and dust with icing sugar.

Store in a sealed container for up to 2 days.

NOTE If you're worried about a soggy bottom, which is more common with pies with wet fillings like this one, you can brush the pastry case with a thin coating of egg yolk before filling, placing it back into the oven for a further 2 minutes to set.

DESSERTS & NO-BAKES

BAKED VANILLA YOGURT
WITH ROASTED PLUMS

SERVES 6–8

I first tried a version of this dish on a weekend away in Somerset. After a disappointing meal at the hotel restaurant, I wasn't expecting much from the dessert, and this one sounded a little boring. Nevertheless, my boyfriend ordered the dish and I, of course, got dessert envy. A vanilla-rich set yogurt topped with roasted fruit – it was a superb summer dish, and so I immediately tried to replicate it when I got back to my own kitchen. This is one of the simplest recipes in the book and also one that I make over and over again, using different seasonal fruits. It may also be the perfect dinner party dessert.

FOR THE ROASTED PLUMS

600g (1lb 5oz) plums (any variety), halved and stoned

3 tablespoons light brown sugar

30g (1oz/2 tablespoons) unsalted butter, diced

3 star anise

seeds from 3 cardamom pods

1 cinnamon stick, broken in half

juice of ½ lemon

FOR THE BAKED VANILLA YOGURT

480ml (17fl oz/2 cups) natural yogurt

397g (14oz) can condensed milk

240ml (8½fl oz/1 cup) double (heavy) cream

seeds scraped from 1 vanilla pod or 2 teaspoons vanilla bean paste

Preheat the oven to 200°C (400°F), Gas Mark 6.

For the roasted plums, place the fruit, cut-side up, into the baking tin and sprinkle over the sugar. Dot the butter and spices throughout the tin, then drizzle over the lemon juice.

Bake for 15–20 minutes, or until the fruit has softened and the skins are starting to wrinkle a little. Carefully transfer the fruit and juices to a heatproof bowl and set aside. (Storing them this way helps the spices infuse into the syrup.)

Wash and dry the baking tin. Reduce the oven temperature to 120°C (250°F), Gas Mark ½.

For the baked yogurt, gently whisk together the yogurt, condensed milk, cream and vanilla seeds or vanilla bean paste in a large bowl. Pour the yogurt mixture into the prepared tin.

Bake for 25–30 minutes, or until the yogurt is just set around the edges and wobbles in the centre. Unlike with cheesecake, the centre will wobble quite significantly, and may even seem a little too loose. Set aside to cool in the tin for 30 minutes, then transfer to the refrigerator and chill for 4 hours.

Once thoroughly chilled, serve scoopfuls of the baked yogurt alongside some of the roasted plums. If you have two 23 x 33cm (9 x 13in) baking tins, or another similar-sized roasting tin, you can also serve the roasted plums hot alongside the chilled baked yogurt, if you prefer.

This dessert is best served on the day it's made.

NOTE These roasted plums work brilliantly with the Masala Chai Baked Rice Pudding on page 123.

MIXED BERRY DUTCH BABY

SERVES 8

As a kid, I loved it when pancake day came round each year. I still do now if I'm being honest. While I enjoy all the wonderful types of pancakes that exist with all the different flavours and toppings, my favourite has always been the simplest, lemon juice and a generous sprinkling of sugar. Dutch Baby pancakes fit into that similarly simple subset served with just some mixed berries and a touch of added drama – it's guaranteed to elicit a great reaction when brought to the table all puffed up like a giant Yorkshire pudding.

4 large eggs

2 tablespoons caster (superfine) sugar

125g (4½oz/1 cup) plain (all-purpose) flour

240ml (8½fl oz/1 cup) whole milk

2 teaspoons vanilla extract

¼ teaspoon fine sea salt

30g (1oz/2 tablespoons) unsalted butter

300g (10½oz) mixed fresh berries, such as raspberries and blueberries

icing (powdered) sugar, for dusting

cream or vanilla ice cream, to serve

Preheat the oven to 220°C (425°F), Gas Mark 7. Place the empty baking tin in the oven while you prepare the batter.

In a large bowl, whisk together the eggs and sugar for 30 seconds to dissolve the sugar, then add the flour, milk, vanilla and salt, whisking to form a smooth, thin batter. Set aside for 20 minutes while the oven heats up.

Remove the hot tin from the oven and add the butter, swirling the tin a little to coat the entire bottom. Pour in the batter, sprinkle over the fruit and bake for about 20 minutes, or until puffed and golden.

Dust with a little sifted icing sugar and serve immediately with a little cream or vanilla ice cream.

This dessert is best served immediately after baking.

NOTE With the fruit baked into the pancake like this, the base of the dish will be a little bit like a thick buttermilk pancake. If you want a thinner base, add the fruit after baking.

STICKY DATE PUDDING
WITH RUM BUTTERSCOTCH SAUCE

SERVES 10–12

If there is one dessert that I'm almost guaranteed to order if I spot it on a menu, it's a sticky toffee pudding. Surely there is nothing better on a cold winter's night than a warming, spiced and sticky date pudding with plenty of rich butterscotch sauce and either cream or, my personal favourite, vanilla ice cream?

FOR THE STICKY DATE PUDDING

120g (4¼oz/8½ tablespoons) unsalted butter, at room temperature, plus extra for greasing

250g (9oz/2 cups) self-raising flour

3 teaspoons ground cinnamon

3 teaspoons ground ginger

1½ teaspoons fine sea salt

250g (9oz/2 cups) stoned dried Medjool dates, diced

1½ teaspoons bicarbonate of soda (baking soda)

85g (3oz/¼ cup) golden syrup or clear honey

220g (8oz/1 cup) light brown sugar

1 teaspoon vanilla extract

3 large eggs

FOR THE BUTTERSCOTCH SAUCE

85g (3oz/6 tablespoons) unsalted butter

150g (5½oz/⅔ cup) light brown sugar

60ml (2¼fl oz/¼ cup) dark rum

½ teaspoon flaked sea salt

1 teaspoon vanilla extract

120ml (4fl oz/½ cup) double (heavy) cream

vanilla ice cream, to serve

Preheat the oven to 180°C (350°F), Gas Mark 4. Lightly grease the baking tin, then line with a large piece of parchment paper so that the excess goes up the sides.

For the pudding, mix the flour, spices and salt in a large bowl and set aside. Place the dates into a medium saucepan and pour over 240ml (8½fl oz/1 cup) water. Bring to a simmer, then cook gently until almost all of the water has evaporated or been absorbed and the dates have softened. Remove from the heat and mix through the bicarbonate of soda.

Place the butter, golden syrup and sugar into a separate large bowl and beat together until light and fluffy using an electric mixer. Beat in the vanilla, then the eggs, one at a time, beating until fully combined before adding another. Fold in the flour mixture until just combined. Scrape the date mixture into the bowl and stir to combine, then scrape into the prepared tin and spread into an even layer.

Bake for 30–35 minutes, or until the pudding springs back to a light touch.

Meanwhile, make the butterscotch sauce. Place the butter and sugar into a medium saucepan and cook over a medium heat until melted and bubbling. Cook for a further 2–3 minutes, to deepen the flavour. Add the rum and cook for 30 seconds, then stir in the salt, vanilla and cream and simmer for a further 3–5 minutes to make a thick but pourable sauce. Set aside until needed.

Leave the pudding to cool for a few minutes before serving warm, topped with the warm butterscotch sauce and a large scoop of vanilla ice cream.

This pudding is best served on the day it's made, but store any leftovers in a sealed container for 3 days and gently reheat the pudding in the oven before serving.

NOTE Any type of dried dates will work, but Medjool dates tend to have the best flavour.

FRESH MINT STRACCIATELLA ICE-CREAM SANDWICHES

SERVES 12

I think it is hard to overstate how impressed people would be should you pull out a batch of these homemade ice-cream sandwiches in the summer – nothing is better when the sun finally raises its head. If you were a fan of mint choc chip ice cream as a child (it was the best flavour after all), this fresh mint ice cream is the grown-up version, and great whether or not you go all the way and make the cookies, too.

You'll need to make this dessert a couple of days before you want to serve it. The custard for the ice cream needs to chill overnight, then the assembled dessert needs to be frozen overnight before serving.

FOR THE FRESH MINT STRACCIATELLA ICE CREAM

400ml (14fl oz/1⅔ cups) double (heavy) cream

360ml (12½floz/1½ cups) whole milk

150g (5½oz/¾ cup) caster (superfine) sugar

1 teaspoon vanilla bean paste

¼ teaspoon fine sea salt

30g (1oz) fresh mint leaves

6 large egg yolks

85g (3oz) dark chocolate (60–70% cocoa solids), roughly chopped

1½ tablespoons extra virgin olive or coconut oil

FOR THE CHOCOLATE WAFER COOKIES

280g (10oz/2¼ cups) plain (all-purpose) flour

40g (1½oz/½ cup) cocoa powder

½ teaspoon bicarbonate of soda

1 teaspoon fine sea salt

200g (7oz/1¾ cups) unsalted butter, at room temperature

125g (4½oz/½ cup + 2 tablespoons) caster (superfine) sugar

125g (4½oz/½ cup + 1 tablespoon) light brown sugar

First, make the custard for the ice cream. Heat the cream, milk, 100g (3½oz/½ cup) of the caster (superfine) sugar, the vanilla and salt in a saucepan until simmering. Remove from the heat and add the mint, then cover and set aside to infuse for 1 hour.

Pour the infused mixture into a large bowl through a fine mesh sieve, pressing on the back of the mint to extract as much liquid as possible, then discard the mint.

Pour the milk mixture back into the pan and bring to a simmer over a medium heat. Meanwhile, whisk the egg yolks and remaining sugar together in a heatproof bowl for a couple of minutes, or until pale. Pour the milk mixture over the eggs, a little at a time, whisking to prevent curdling. Return the custard to the pan and cook, stirring constantly, until it coats the back of a wooden spoon or registers 75–80°C/170–175°F on a thermometer.

Pour the finished custard into a heatproof bowl and cool over a bowl of iced water, stirring occasionally until cool. Cover and refrigerate overnight.

The next day, make the cookies. Mix together the flour, cocoa, bicarbonate of soda and salt in a bowl. Place the butter and both sugars in a separate large bowl and beat together using an electric mixer for 3–4 minutes, or until light and creamy. Add the flour mixture and mix briefly just until it starts to form a uniform dough (don't mix for too long, otherwise the cookies will be tough and chewy). Tip out on to a work surface and use your hands to bring it together into a dough. Divide in half and form each portion into a flat rectangle. Wrap both in clingfilm and refrigerate for about 1 hour, or until firm.

Preheat the oven to 180°C (350°F), Gas Mark 4.

CONTINUED OVERLEAF

Working with one piece of dough at a time, roll it out between two sheets of parchment paper into a 23 x 33cm (9 x 13in) rectangle. Peel off the top sheet and trim the excess dough if needed, then cut the bottom sheet of parchment paper so that it just sits neatly underneath the dough. Carefully lift into the baking tin with the parchment paper. Use a knife to score into 12 cookies (three rows of four) and dock each a couple of times with a fork. Pop the tin into the freezer for 10 minutes before baking.

Bake for 17–20 minutes or until firm around the edges but just a little soft in the middle. Leave the cookies to cool completely in the tin, then transfer to a wire rack. Repeat with the second sheet of dough. (If you have two 23 x 33cm/9 x 13in tins you can bake both at the same time.)

Next, finish the ice cream. Pour the chilled custard into an ice-cream machine and churn following the manufacturer's instructions.

Meanwhile, melt the chocolate and oil together in a heatproof bowl set over a pan of simmering water (ensuring the bottom of the bowl doesn't touch the water underneath). As the ice cream finishes churning, pour the chocolate mixture into the machine in a steady stream. It will freeze instantly, forming little shards of chocolate.

To assemble the dessert, place one sheet of the wafer cookies in the bottom of the baking tin. Spread the ice cream over this bottom layer of cookies in an even layer, then place the second sheet of cookies on top and press into the ice cream. Wrap the tin in clingfilm and freeze overnight before serving.

To serve, cut into 12 portions using a sharp, serrated knife. Store in a sealed container in the freezer for 2–3 weeks.

NOTE If you don't have an ice-cream machine you can always skip making the ice cream and use a shop bought version, letting the ice cream soften before spreading between the sheets of cookie as in the recipe.

MANGO AND LIME MERINGUE ROULADE

SERVES 8

Roulades have a reputation for being tricky, prone to cracking and hard to roll. Thankfully, with a meringue roulade any imperfections are part of the charm. The base meringue recipe is a great kicking off point and you can fill it with whatever fruit is in season. I love this in summer because it takes no time to make and is lighter than many other desserts.

unsalted butter or neutral-tasting oil, for greasing

icing (powdered) sugar, for dusting

FOR THE MERINGUE

3 large egg whites

⅛ teaspoon cream of tartar

175g (6oz/¾ cup + 2 tablespoons) caster (superfine) sugar

1 teaspoon vanilla bean paste

finely grated zest of 1 lime

1 teaspoon cornflour (cornstarch)

35g (1¼oz/½ cup) coconut flakes (untoasted)

FOR THE FILLING AND TOPPING

300ml (10fl oz/1¼ cups) double (heavy) cream

1 teaspoon vanilla bean paste

1 large ripe mango

100g (3½oz) white chocolate, melted and cooled

Preheat the oven to 180°C (350°F), Gas Mark 4. Lightly grease the baking tin, then line with a large piece of parchment paper so that the excess goes up the sides.

For the meringue, place the egg whites and cream of tartar into a large bowl. Using an electric mixer, whisk on medium speed until the egg whites start to foam, then slowly add the sugar, a tablespoon at a time. Once all the sugar has been added, increase the speed to high and whisk until the meringue holds stiff, glossy peaks. Add the vanilla, lime zest and cornflour and whisk briefly to combine. Scrape the meringue into the prepared tin and spread into an even layer, then scatter over the coconut flakes.

Bake for 25–30 minutes, or until lightly browned and firm to the touch. If the coconut browns faster than the meringue, tent the tin with a sheet of foil.

Remove the meringue from the oven and immediately turn it out on to another sheet of parchment paper, then peel off the lining paper. Transfer to a wire rack (on the paper) and leave to cool completely.

For the filling, whip the cream and vanilla together in a bowl until it holds soft peaks, then set aside. Peel, stone and cut the mango into thin slivers.

To assemble, drizzle the melted chocolate over the meringue and arrange the mango slices evenly across the top. Spread the whipped cream over the fruit and then carefully roll up into a tight spiral, not worrying if the meringue cracks slightly. To finish, dust with a little icing sugar. Cut into slices to serve.

This roulade is best served on the day it's made.

FLOURLESS CHOCOLATE MERINGUE CAKE

SERVES 12–16

When is cake dessert and when is dessert cake? I don't know how to tell you the difference, but I can spot the difference when I see it. This recipe uses a flourless chocolate cake as its base, but with the meringue topping, it's absolutely a dessert. The mixture of the melt-in-the-mouth chocolate cake and the light and crisp meringue makes for a textural dream. To finish the cake off, I have included chopped hazelnuts, but you could also make a wonderful pistachio version instead, if you like.

FOR THE FLOURLESS CHOCOLATE CAKE

250g (9oz/2 sticks + 2 tablespoons) unsalted butter, diced, plus extra for greasing

250g (9oz) dark chocolate (70–75% cocoa solids), roughly chopped

6 large eggs

50g (1¾oz/¼ cup) caster (superfine) sugar

165g (5¾oz/¾ cup) light brown sugar

¼ teaspoon fine sea salt

85g (3oz/¾ cup) roasted hazelnuts, finely chopped

FOR THE COCOA MERINGUE TOPPING

3 large egg whites

pinch of fine sea salt

200g (7oz/1 cup) caster (superfine) sugar

2 tablespoons cocoa powder

cream and cacao nibs, to serve (optional)

NOTE To make a mocha version, reduce the cocoa in the meringue by half and replace with a tablespoon of instant espresso powder.

Preheat the oven to 180°C (350°F), Gas Mark 4. Lightly grease the baking tin and line with a piece of parchment paper that goes up the sides of the tin.

For the chocolate cake, place the butter and chocolate into a heatproof bowl and melt, either in a microwave, using short bursts of heat to prevent it from burning, or set over a pan of simmering water (ensuring the bottom of the bowl doesn't touch the water underneath). Remove from the heat and set aside to cool slightly.

Place the eggs, both sugars and the salt into another large bowl and, using an electric mixer, whisk on medium-high speed for 7–8 minutes, or until pale and tripled in volume. Add the hazelnuts, reserving a couple of tablespoons to decorate, and gently fold into the mixture.

Pour the egg mixture over the cooled chocolate mixture, in three additions, and fold together until combined and streak-free. Pour into the prepared tin and gently level out. Bake for 30 minutes.

When the cake has been in the oven for 25 minutes, make the meringue topping. Place the egg whites and salt into a spotlessly clean bowl (glass or metal is preferable) and whisk until the meringue is foamy, then slowly add the sugar, a spoonful at a time. Continue whisking until the meringue holds stiff, glossy peaks.

Gently spread the meringue over the top, being careful not to crush the cake underneath. Dust the cocoa over the meringue and lightly swirl together. Bake for a further 25 minutes or until the meringue is crisp.

Leave the cake to cool in the tin for at least an hour before transferring to a serving plate. Serve in slices with a little drizzle of cream and a sprinkling of cacao nibs.

Store covered for up to 2 days.

KEY LIME PIE WITH SPECULOOS CRUST

SERVES 10–12

Should this recipe actually be in the pastries, pies and tarts chapter? Possibly, but I have always thought of this dish, especially in this form, as a dessert. Regardless of its identity, we can all agree that key lime pie is one of those summer desserts we continually turn to, even if you can't get actual key limes.

This recipe is a breeze to make and the flavour is incredible – the condensed milk adds an almost caramelized note to the bright citrusy limes, and it's a perennial crowd-pleaser. For my version, I have changed one little thing, the choice of biscuit for the base. Instead of digestives or graham crackers, I have gone with speculoos or Lotus biscuits. They really enhance the toasty caramelized notes of the pie.

FOR THE BASE

370g (13oz) speculoos or Lotus biscuits, finely crushed

85g (3oz/6 tablespoons) unsalted butter, melted

1 large egg white

¼ teaspoon fine sea salt

FOR THE FILLING

6 large egg yolks

finely grated zest of 2 limes

300ml (10fl oz/1¼ cups) lime juice (from 8–10 large limes)

2 x 397g (14oz) cans condensed milk

FOR THE TOPPING

480ml (17fl oz/2 cups) double (heavy) cream

1 tablespoon finely grated lime zest

Preheat the oven to 180°C (350°F), Gas Mark 4.

For the base, mix together the biscuit crumbs, melted butter, egg white and salt, and then press into the base and up the sides of the baking tin. Use a glass or a measuring cup to really compact the base so it's nice and solid.

Bake for 15–18 minutes, or until the base has darkened slightly and smells nice and toasty. If the base puffs up as it bakes, lightly press it back into place using a glass. Remove from the oven and reduce the oven temperature to 160°C (325°F), Gas Mark 3.

For the filling, whisk all the ingredients together in a bowl until fully combined, then pour evenly into the crust.

Bake for 30–35 minutes, or until just set around the edges and with a gentle wobble in the middle. Leave to cool for an hour, then chill in the refrigerator for at least 3 hours before serving.

For the topping, whip the cream in a bowl until it just starts to hold its shape. Slice the pie and serve each portion with a dollop of cream and a sprinkling of lime zest.

Store covered in the refrigerator for up to 3 days.

STRAWBERRY AND RHUBARB COBBLER

SERVES 12

My all-time favourite pie is made with that glorious combination of rhubarb and strawberries. The only problem? Making this pie in the UK isn't as simple as it seems. The best rhubarb comes into season early on in the year, but by the time the strawberries appear at the market, rhubarb has all but disappeared, or it's thick, green and stringy, which is not what I'm looking for. However, when the stars align and by some miracle the two cross over, I make pie, and when a pie is too much effort, I make cobbler, all the joy, half the work. The topping for this recipe also happens to be gluten-free, using a blend of oat flour, ground almonds and rice flour.

FOR THE FRUIT FILLING

680g (1lb 8oz) fresh rhubarb, cut into 2.5cm (1in) pieces

680g (1lb 8oz) fresh strawberries, hulled and halved

1 teaspoon vanilla bean paste

juice of 1 lemon

200g (7oz/1 cup) caster (superfine) sugar

5 tablespoons ground arrowroot or cornflour (cornstarch)

FOR THE DROP SCONES

125g (4½oz/1⅓ cups + 1 tablespoon) oat flour

125g (4½oz/1¼ cups + 1 tablespoon) ground almonds

100g (3½oz/⅔ cup) rice flour

150g (5½oz/¾ cup) caster (superfine) sugar

2½ teaspoons baking powder

¾ teaspoon fine sea salt

125g (4½oz/1 stick + 1 tablespoon) unsalted butter, diced and chilled

160ml (5½fl oz/⅔ cup) buttermilk

demerara sugar, for sprinkling

vanilla ice cream, to serve (optional)

Preheat the oven to 190°C (375°F), Gas Mark 5.

For the filling, place the fruit into the baking tin and toss together with the vanilla and lemon juice. In a small bowl, mix together the caster sugar and arrowroot or cornflour. Sprinkle this mixture over the fruit and toss together to combine. Set aside while you make the drop scone mixture.

In a large bowl, mix together the oat flour, ground almonds, rice flour, caster sugar, baking powder and salt. Add the butter and toss together to coat in the flour mixture. Using your fingertips, rub the butter into the flour mixture until it resembles uneven breadcrumbs. Pour in the buttermilk, using a round-bladed knife to stir it into the breadcrumb mixture until evenly combined. Using a large spoon or spring-loaded ice-cream scoop, dollop the drop scone mixture atop the fruit and then sprinkle with demerara sugar.

Bake for 45 minutes, or until the scones are golden brown and the filling is bubbling. If the scones are browning too quickly, tent the cobbler with a sheet of foil partway through baking.

Leave the cobbler to cool for 10 minutes or so before serving each portion with a scoop of vanilla ice cream, if you like.

This cobbler is best eaten warm on the day it's made.

ESPRESSO CHOCOFLAN

SERVES 15

Not just cake, not just flan, but a glorious mixture of the two. This dessert, which originally goes by the name of chocoflan or impossible cake, is a wonder of baking science. A wonder because, as the dessert bakes, the two layers somehow manage to switch positions. The cake is spread into the tin first with the flan then carefully poured on top, but when it's removed from the oven, the cake is magically now on top and the flan has seeped its way through the cake batter and settled on the base of the tin. Traditionally, the flavours are kept to caramel for the flan and chocolate for the cake, but I have snuck a little coffee into the flan.

FOR THE CARAMEL TOPPING

200g (7oz/1 cup) caster (superfine) sugar

FOR THE CHOCOLATE CAKE LAYER

60g (2¼oz/4 tablespoons) unsalted butter, at room temperature, plus extra for greasing

150g (5½oz/¾ cup) light brown sugar

1 large egg

125g (4½oz/1 cup) plain (all-purpose) flour

35g (1¼oz/⅓ cup) cocoa powder

½ teaspoon baking powder

1 teaspoon bicarbonate of soda

½ teaspoon fine sea salt

120ml (4fl oz/½ cup) sour cream

80ml (3fl oz/⅓ cup) boiling water

FOR THE COFFEE FLAN

410g (14½oz can) evaporated milk

397g (14oz can) condensed milk

100g (3½oz) cream cheese, at room temperature

5 large eggs

1 teaspoon vanilla extract

4 teaspoons instant espresso powder

100g (3½oz) pecans, roughly chopped

Preheat the oven to 180°C (350°F), Gas Mark 4. Lightly grease the baking tin and line the base with parchment paper.

For the caramel, place the caster sugar in a small saucepan. Cook over a medium heat, without stirring, until the sugar has dissolved and caramelized, turning a rich golden brown. Immediately pour the caramel into the prepared tin and swirl to coat the base. Set aside.

For the cake, place the butter and brown sugar in a bowl and beat together using an electric mixer until light and fluffy, about 5 minutes. Add the egg and beat until combined. In a separate bowl, sift together the flour, cocoa, baking powder, bicarbonate of soda and salt. Mix the dry ingredients into the butter mixture in two additions, adding the sour cream in between. Once the cake batter is smooth, add the boiling water and mix briefly to combine, then transfer to the baking tin, spreading evenly.

For the flan, place all the ingredients in a blender and blend until smooth and combined. Pour the mixture gently on top of the cake batter. I find it easier to pour the flan mixture over the back of a spoon so that it lands gently on the cake. Tent the baking tin with a layer of foil and place in a large roasting tin, then fill with boiling water so it reaches about halfway up the sides of the baking tin.

Carefully place the roasting tin into the oven and bake for 1 hour–1 hour 10 minutes, or until a knife inserted into the middle of the cake comes out clean.

Leave the cake to cool fully while still resting in the water bath. Once cooled, remove the tin from the water bath, wrap in clingfilm and refrigerate for 4 hours. (While the cake needs at least 4 hours to chill, you can leave it overnight if you want to prepare ahead.)

To serve, run a knife around the edge of the tin to loosen the cake and carefully invert it on to a large serving platter. If the cake doesn't immediately come out of the tin, gently warm the base of the tin over a gas hob for 30 seconds or so.

Cut into slices to serve. This is best served within 1–2 days of baking (keep it wrapped in the refrigerator) and within a day once turned out.

MASALA CHAI BAKED RICE PUDDING

SERVES 10

As a child, rice pudding was one of my favourite dishes, it was warming, pure comfort, and even though it's so simple it feels almost luxurious with soft, tender rice and a rich, vanilla-heavy, almost custard-like sauce. This version amps up the idea of comfort using flavours from one of my favourite drinks, a spiced masala chai, which adds a whole host of warming spices, with a result that is just crying out for a cold, wintery night and an open fire. I don't have an open fire, so the rice pudding will just have to do. This is delicious on its own, but if you prefer you can serve it with some roasted plums (see page 104).

45g (1¾oz/3 tablespoons) unsalted butter

seeds scraped from 1 vanilla pod

seeds from 3 cardamom pods, ground

2 teaspoons ground cinnamon

1 star anise

2 cloves

3 slices of peeled fresh root ginger

150g (5½oz/1 cup) pudding rice or other medium-grain rice

1.5 litres (2¾ pints) whole milk

180ml (6½fl oz/¾ cup) double (heavy) cream

100g (3½oz/⅓ cup + 2 tablespoons) light brown sugar

roasted plums (see page 104) to serve – optional

Preheat the oven to 150°C (300°F), Gas Mark 2. Lightly grease the baking tin with a little bit of the butter.

Heat the remaining butter in a small saucepan over a medium heat until melted and starting to sizzle. Add the vanilla seeds, spices and fresh ginger and cook for 2 minutes to help infuse the spiced flavour into the butter. Stir in the rice, then stir in the milk, cream and sugar. Pour this mixture into the prepared tin and mix a little so everything is evenly distributed.

Bake for 1½–2 hours, or until the rice is tender and the liquid has been absorbed. Now to be honest, I don't like the skin that develops with a baked rice pudding, so after the first hour I like to stir it every 15–20 minutes to prevent a skin from forming. However, if you're one of those people who does love it, stir once or twice during baking, leaving it untouched for the final hour. After 1½ hours have passed, check the texture of the pudding, if you like it looser you may want to take it out at this stage, but if you like it thicker then leave it in for the full 2 hours.

Remove the whole spices and cool slightly, before serving warm.

I prefer to serve this on the day it's made, but if you have leftovers, you can store these in a sealed container in the refrigerator and serve chilled – the leftovers will keep for 2 days.

TIRAMISU

SERVES 8-10

Tiramisu may have gone in and out of fashion multiple times, but my love for the dish is unwavering. It also happens to be one of those desserts that is stupidly quick and easy to pull together.

Classically, the dessert is made with Marsala, an Italian fortified wine, but as it's something I never have in the house, I prefer to use a dark rum instead (if you only have a spiced rum, this also works). While the making of the dish is the work of minutes, to serve it at its best it needs a few hours rest in the refrigerator before serving, and can actually happily sit in there for a day if you really want to get ahead.

4 large eggs, separated

100g (3½oz/½ cup) caster (superfine) sugar

500g (1lb 2oz/2¼ cups) mascarpone at room temperature

1 teaspoon vanilla bean paste

pinch of fine sea salt

240ml (8½fl oz/1 cup) hot strong coffee

120ml (4fl oz/½ cup) dark rum

400g (14oz) sponge fingers, preferably Savoiardi

dark chocolate, for grating (optional)

cocoa powder, for dusting

Place the egg yolks in a large bowl with the sugar (reserving a couple of tablespoons for the whites) and whisk together using an electric mixer for 3–4 minutes, or until very pale and increased in volume. Add the mascarpone and vanilla and whisk for a couple of minutes until smooth.

Add the egg whites to a separate large, clean bowl along with the pinch of salt and, using the electric mixer (clean the whisk first), whisk until the mixture is foaming. Slowly add the reserved sugar, a little bit at a time, whisking until the whites hold medium peaks. Working in three additions, fold the whites into the mascarpone mixture until smooth and creamy.

To assemble the dessert, pour the coffee and rum into a wide, shallow bowl and stir together. Dip the sponge fingers into the coffee mixture, allowing them to soak for 10 seconds or so, and then layer half into the bottom of the baking tin. Depending on the brand of sponge fingers, you may need to break up a couple to create a uniform layer. Add half of the mascarpone mixture and spread into an even layer. If you like, you can grate over a little dark chocolate at this point. Repeat this layering a second time with the remaining soaked sponge fingers and mascarpone mixture, finishing with a generous dusting of cocoa powder.

Refrigerate the tiramisu for at least 4 hours (or for up to a day) before serving.

Store in a sealed container in the refrigerator for up to 2 days.

NOTE If you want to make this even more special, you can heat a little chocolate hazelnut spread and drizzle it over each layer of soaked sponge fingers, just don't be overly generous as it makes the dessert a lot richer (you'll also want to serve slightly smaller portions). I first had a tiramisu like this at Da Enzo in Rome and it was one of the best versions of the dessert I have ever had.

DESSERTS & NO-BAKES

BOURBON BANANA BREAD PUDDING

SERVES 8–10

Bread pudding is one of those desserts we all know and love, it's easy to throw together and is a great comforting winter dish. I make mine with brioche for its buttery flavour and light texture. I have also added bananas and bourbon to make something reminiscent of the banana custard I loved as a child, but a slightly more grown-up version. I like to serve this with a cold crème anglaise, but it is equally good with a splash of cream or a scoop of vanilla ice cream.

450g (1lb) brioche loaf

unsalted butter, for greasing

600ml (20fl oz/2½ cups) whole milk

120ml (4fl oz/½ cup) maple syrup

60ml (2¼fl oz/¼ cup) bourbon or whiskey

4 large eggs

1 tablespoon vanilla extract

3 large bananas, peeled and sliced

100g (3½oz/¾ cup) pecans, roughly chopped

demerara sugar, for sprinkling

cream, vanilla ice cream or chilled crème anglaise, to serve

Because it is unlikely you just have a loaf of brioche lying around, going stale, we're going to dry it out a little before baking. Cut the brioche into 2.5cm (1in) cubes, place on a wire rack and set aside for a couple of hours to dry out slightly. If you have the time, this is best done overnight.

When you are ready to make the pudding, lightly grease the baking tin with butter.

To make the custard, whisk together the milk, maple syrup, bourbon or whiskey, eggs and vanilla in a bowl until combined. Add the brioche pieces to the prepared tin along with the sliced bananas and chopped pecans, tossing together to combine. Pour over the custard, then set the tin aside for 30–40 minutes, pressing down on the brioche occasionally, to encourage it to soak up the custard.

Preheat the oven to 180°C (350°F), Gas Mark 4.

Before you bake the pudding, sprinkle it liberally with demerara sugar. Bake for 40–45 minutes, or until a knife inserted into the pudding comes out clean.

Leave to cool for a few minutes before serving warm, topped with cream, ice cream or my favourite, a thin chilled crème anglaise.

Because of the fresh bananas, this bread pudding is best served on the day it's made.

SOUR CHERRY & LEMON ICE-BOX CAKE

SERVES 12

Sour cherries seem to be an elusive fruit. Finding them fresh in the supermarket is nigh on impossible and finding them at a greengrocer or farmers' market seems almost as hard. Thankfully, the frozen variety is a little easier to track down and I hoard them when I see them. I would encourage you to get your hands on some for this dessert. You can use regular sweet cherries, but the flavour won't be quite the same, so double the lemon juice, reduce the sugar a little and add a few drops of almond extract to get you close. You can either freeze this, akin to a semifreddo, which is my preference, or simply chill it in the refrigerator, which will, of course, give it a softer finish.

unsalted butter or neutral-tasting oil, for greasing

FOR THE SOUR CHERRY COMPOTE

600g (1lb 5oz) frozen pitted sour cherries, defrosted

120ml (4fl oz/½ cup) kirsch

100g (3½oz/½ cup) caster (superfine) sugar

juice of ½ lemon

2 tablespoons cornflour (cornstarch)

FOR THE FILLING

250g (9oz/1⅛ cups) mascarpone, at room temperature

35g (1¼oz/¼ cup) icing (powdered) sugar

800ml (28fl oz/3⅓ cups) double (heavy) cream

1 teaspoon vanilla bean paste

150g (5½oz/½ cup) lemon curd

270g (9¾oz) digestives, graham crackers or speculoos biscuits

Lightly grease the baking tin and line the base with parchment paper. If you want to remove the cake from the tin to serve, you can line the tin with a piece of parchment paper that overhangs the two long sides.

For the cherry compote, place the cherries, kirsch, sugar and lemon juice into a large saucepan and cook over a medium-high heat for about 5 minutes, until the fruit softens and releases a lot of juice. Use a slotted spoon to remove the cherries to a heatproof bowl, leaving the syrup in the pan. Continue cooking the syrup until it is reduced to about 240ml (8½fl oz/1 cup).

Place the cornflour in a small bowl and whisk in a little of the cherry syrup to form a smooth paste. Add this to the cherry syrup in the pan and simmer, stirring, for a couple of minutes, or until slightly thickened. Pour the syrup over the fruit, cool slightly, then cover with clingfilm and refrigerate until cool.

For the filling, whisk together the mascarpone, icing sugar, 600ml (20fl oz/2½cups) of the cream and the vanilla in a bowl until the mixture just starts to hold its shape. Add the lemon curd and continue whisking until the mixture holds soft peaks.

To assemble the dessert, spread a thin layer of the lemon cream over the base of the prepared tin, then cover with a layer of biscuits, breaking them up as needed. Spread over half of the remaining lemon cream and then dollop over about a third of the cherry compote. Repeat the layering a second time and then finish with a final layer of biscuits.

Cover the tin with clingfilm and refrigerate or freeze for at least 4 hours before serving.

Just before serving, whip the remaining cream to soft peaks and spread over the dessert. Cut into slices and serve each portion with a spoonful of the remaining compote.

Store in a sealed container in the freezer for up to 2 weeks; if refrigerated, it will keep for 3–4 days.

BURNT BASQUE CHEESECAKE

SERVES 16–18

In my book, there are few desserts that can equal a classic cheesecake, but the worry about it cracking, having to use a water bath and also wrapping the tin in foil mean it's a bit of a faff to make. This is why I love the 'to hell with it' approach of a Basque cheesecake. You purposefully bake it until dark, almost burnt, it's quick to make and is basically foolproof. Obviously, cheesecake is rich and this is a large one that feeds a crowd, so I love to serve it alongside the sour cherry compote from my Sour Cherry & Lemon Ice-box Cake recipe (see page 128).

unsalted butter or neutral-tasting oil, for greasing

1.2kg (2lb 10oz) full-fat cream cheese, at room temperature

400g (14oz/2 cups) caster (superfine) sugar

7 large eggs

1 teaspoon fine sea salt

1 tablespoon vanilla extract

360ml (12½fl oz/1½ cups) double (heavy) cream

30g (1oz/4 tablespoons) plain (all-purpose) flour

Preheat the oven to 220°C (425°F), Gas Mark 7. Lightly grease the baking tin and line with a large sheet of parchment paper, so that it lines the base and sides, reaching up above the sides of the tin.

In a large bowl, beat together the cream cheese and sugar with an electric mixer until smooth. Add the eggs, one at a time, scraping down as needed and mixing until combined. Add the salt, vanilla and cream and mix briefly until fully combined. Sift over the flour and mix briefly to combine. Pour into the prepared tin and level out.

Bake for about 40 minutes, or until dark, almost burnt. The cheesecake will have quite a wobble at this stage.

Leave to cool completely in the tin. You can either let it cool to room temperature, which will result in a softer creamier texture, or you can let it cool at room temperature for an hour before chilling in the refrigerator for a minimum of 4 hours. This will result in a denser texture, a little more like a traditional cheesecake. Whichever way you cool the cheesecake, it will collapse on itself as it sits – that's to be expected, so don't worry about it.

Remove from the tin and cut into portions to serve.

Store covered in the refrigerator for around 3–4 days.

BUNS & BREADS

ESPRESSO CACAO NIB MORNING BUNS

MAKES 6

This recipe is an ode to San Francisco, partly inspired by the 'Morning Bun' at the legendary Tartine Bakery, and partly by the 'nibby sticky buns' served at Dandelion Chocolate, two wonderful recipes from two of my favourite San Francisco sweet spots. Instead of a more difficult croissant dough, this uses a simpler brioche dough made with a coffee compound butter, a nod to the bay area's seeming obsession with all things caffeinated.

1 batch of brioche dough (see page 152 – made with just 75g/2¾oz/²/₃ stick unsalted butter)

plain (all-purpose) flour, for dusting

1 egg yolk, beaten, for glazing

FOR THE COFFEE BUTTER

150g (5½oz/1 stick + 1½ tablespoons) unsalted butter, at room temperature

1 heaped tablespoon instant espresso powder

FOR THE COATING

100g (3½oz/½ cup) caster (superfine) sugar

1 tablespoon cacao nibs

1 teaspoon instant espresso powder

NOTE The brioche dough needs to chill overnight, so start this recipe the day before you want to bake it.

Make the brioche dough according to the instructions on page 152, then press into a flat disc, cover with clingfilm and refrigerate overnight.

For the coffee butter, beat the butter in a bowl using an electric mixer or a wooden spoon until soft and creamy. Mix in the espresso powder. Draw a 20cm (8in) square on a piece of parchment paper and turn it over. Scrape the butter into the middle of the square and spread into an even layer within the lines. Fold the parchment paper over to enclose the butter and neaten with a rolling pin. Refrigerate overnight and remove the espresso butter from the refrigerator 10–15 minutes before the brioche dough to soften it slightly.

Roll out the brioche dough on a lightly floured work surface into a 20 x 40cm (8 x 16in) rectangle. Place the espresso butter on one side of the dough and fold the second side up and over the butter. Pinch the seams together to enclose the butter. Gently press the dough with a rolling pin to flatten it a little before rolling out into a 20 x 50cm (8 x 20in) rectangle. Fold the dough in thirds like a business letter, then wrap in clingfilm and refrigerate for 30 minutes. Repeat this rolling, folding and chilling twice more, refrigerating for a final 30 minutes. Meanwhile, line the base of the baking tin with a piece of parchment paper.

Roll out the finished dough into an 18 x 28cm (7 x 11in) rectangle. Trim the edges and cut into six even squares. Place the buns into the prepared baking tin, cover with cling film and set aside in a warm place until the buns have almost doubled in size, about 1 hour.

Preheat the oven to 200°C (400°F), Gas Mark 6.

Brush the top of the buns with the beaten egg yolk, then bake for 15 minutes or until golden. Pulse the sugar, cacao nibs and espresso powder in a food processor until finely ground.

Leave to cool in the tin for 10 minutes, before tossing in the cacao nib sugar.

Best served warm on the same day, but these buns will keep for 1–2 days in a sealed container.

OVERNIGHT CRÈME BRÛLÉE FRENCH TOAST

SERVES 6

My family has a small tradition that on the morning after Christmas Day, I make brunch for everyone. This normally ends up being a big batch of pancakes or waffles, and while I love those dishes, making them for a big group of people is not really my favourite way to spend the morning. I'm definitely not the best short order cook, and by the time I sit down for brunch, everyone else has long finished. Thankfully, this overnight French toast solves all of those problems; with just a couple of minutes work the night before, a very special brunch awaits you in the morning, easily made before you've even poured that all-important first mug of coffee.

FOR THE FRENCH TOAST

6 slices of brioche, each 2.5cm (1in) thick

unsalted butter or neutral-tasting oil, for greasing

6 large eggs

240ml (8½fl oz/1 cup) whole milk

60g (2¼oz/5 tablespoons) caster (superfine) sugar, plus extra for the brûlée topping

2 teaspoons vanilla extract

FOR THE BAKED BLUEBERRY COMPOTE

150g (5½oz/1½ cups) fresh blueberries

2 tablespoons caster (superfine) sugar

juice of ½ lemon

crème fraîche, to serve

To enable the brioche to absorb as much of the custard mixture as possible, it's best if the bread is stale. Place the brioche slices on a wire rack a few hours before you want to prepare the dish to dry.

For the French toast, lightly grease a 23 x 33cm (9 x 13in) baking tin and line the base with a piece of parchment paper.

To make the custard, add the eggs, milk, sugar and vanilla to a large bowl and whisk together until combined. Working with one slice of brioche at a time, dip and soak the bread in the custard for a minute or so, until the bread is saturated. Arrange the soaked slices of brioche in the prepared tin, then if there is any excess custard, pour this over the bread. Cover the tin with clingfilm and refrigerate overnight.

The next morning, preheat the oven to 180°C (350°F), Gas Mark 4.

Unwrap the tin and bake for about 30 minutes, flipping the brioche slices over halfway through cooking, until a knife inserted into the middle of the bread feels hot to the touch and comes out clean.

When it comes to the compote the easiest method is to bake it alongside the French toast. Place the ingredients in a small roasting dish, stir together a little and then bake alongside for about 20 minutes, or until the berries have released juice and started to sag but are not fully broken down. Alternatively, to make on the hob, place the ingredients in a medium-sized saucepan and cook over a low-medium heat, stirring occasionally, for 8–10 minutes, or until juicy and starting to break down. Set aside to cool slightly before serving.

Remove the tin from the oven and preheat your grill (broiler) to high. Sprinkle each slice of French toast with a thin layer of sugar, about 2 teaspoons per slice. Pop the tin under the hot grill for 2–3 minutes, or until the sugar has melted and caramelized, taking it as dark as you like.

The edges of the French toast will caramelize and brown a little, but this is a wonderful thing.

Serve each portion of the French toast topped with a dollop of crème fraîche and a generous spoonful of the compote.

FAT TUESDAY FINGER BUNS

MAKES 8

When spring arrives and the chill of winter finally wears off, the day I look forward to the most is Fat Tuesday, the Scandinavian term for Shrove Tuesday (pancake day for my fellow Brits). Instead of pancakes, I often partake in the Swedish treat of Semla, a cardamom bun filled with marzipan and whipped cream. This recipe is a bit of a Franken recipe, mashing together those Swedish Semlor buns and Finnish Laskiaispulla (which use jam instead of the almond paste), with a nod to an old British classic, Dorset cream split buns. The bread dough is infused with the light perfume of cardamom and filled with a mix of marzipan and blueberry jam, finished, of course, with lightly whipped cream and a generous dusting of icing sugar.

FOR THE BUNS

1 batch of Japanese Milk Bread (see page 161)

2 teaspoons ground cardamom

1 egg, beaten with a splash of milk, for glazing

icing (powdered) sugar, for dusting

FOR THE FILLING

200g (7oz) marzipan

180ml (6½fl oz/¾ cup) whole milk

160g (5¾oz/8 tablespoons) blueberry jam

600ml (20fl oz/2½ cups) double (heavy) cream

1 teaspoon vanilla bean paste

Line the base of the baking tin with a piece of parchment paper.

Make the bread dough according to the instructions on page 161 with the cardamom added to the flour. Once the dough has risen for the first time, tip it out on to a lightly floured work surface, knock back and divide into eight equal-sized pieces. Form each piece of dough into a ball, then roll each one into a sausage shape about 14cm (5½in) long. Place the sausages of dough into the prepared baking tin, in two rows of four. Cover the tin with cling film and set aside in a warm place for about an hour until almost doubled in size.

Preheat the oven to 190°C (375°F), Gas Mark 5.

Brush the top of the buns with the egg and milk glaze. Bake for 18–20 minutes, or until golden brown. Leave to cool in the tin for a few minutes before carefully transferring the buns to a wire rack to cool completely.

Once cool, use a serrated knife to cut the buns in half widthways. Set the tops aside, then use your fingers to scoop out about a third of the inside of each bun, placing the crumbs in a bowl. Crumble the marzipan into the bowl, add the milk and mix together to form a paste. Spread the marzipan paste back into the bottoms of the buns, then spread a thin layer of the blueberry jam on top.

Whip the cream and vanilla together in a large bowl until it holds soft peaks. Spoon or pipe the cream on top of the jam and then place the bun tops back on. Dust with a little sifted icing sugar and serve.

Kept in a sealed container, the unfilled buns will keep for 2–3 days, but once filled, they are best served on the day made.

CHOCOLATE TAHINI BABKA BUNS

MAKES 12

Tahini has become one of those ingredients I try to sneak into each and every recipe I can. If I'd let myself, this would be a cookbook entirely devoted to tahini recipes. I've also had a love affair with babka for more than a few years, but it wasn't until I visited Tel Aviv and spent the day with Uri Scheft of Lehamim Bakery that the idea of mashing the two things together came to mind, the tahini adding a nutty, slightly savoury note to the rich chocolate filling we all know and love. On that trip, I ate tahini every single day, and come to think of it, I probably ate babka every day, too!

FOR THE BABKA DOUGH

500g (1lb 2oz/4 cups) strong white bread flour, plus extra for dusting

25g (1oz/⅛ cup) caster (superfine) sugar

1 teaspoon fine sea salt

7g (¼oz) fast-action dried yeast

250ml (9fl oz/1 cup + 2 teaspoons) whole milk

2 large eggs

100g (3½oz/7 tablespoons) unsalted butter, at room temperature, diced, plus extra for greasing

FOR THE CHOCOLATE TAHINI FILLING

100g (3½oz) dark chocolate (65–70% cocoa solids), finely chopped

100g (3½oz/7 tablespoons) unsalted butter, diced

55g (2oz/¼ cup) light brown sugar

100g (3½oz/⅓ cup) tahini

flaked sea salt, for sprinkling

FOR THE SYRUP

65g (2½oz/⅓ cup) caster (superfine) sugar

1 teaspoon vanilla extract

2 teaspoons sesame seeds

For the bread dough, make a batch of brioche using the ingredients listed here with the instructions on page 144. Tip the dough into a lightly greased large bowl, cover with clingfilm and refrigerate overnight or for up to 2 days.

The next day, lightly grease or line the base of the baking tin with a piece of parchment paper. Make the filling. Place the chocolate and butter in a heatproof bowl set over a pan of simmering water (ensuring the bottom of the bowl doesn't touch the water underneath) until melted. Remove from the heat, stir in the brown sugar and tahini, then set aside.

Remove the dough from the refrigerator and, working on a lightly floured surface, roll out into a large 50 x 50cm (20 x 20in) square. Spread the chocolate tahini mixture evenly over the dough. At this point, the tahini mixture will be loose and glossy, so if you attempt to roll the dough up now it will be very messy, therefore, allow the mixture to sit for a couple of minutes until it goes a little tackier and loses its shine (don't leave this too long though, because the filling will eventually set, meaning it won't stick to the dough when it's rolled). Sprinkle over a little flaked sea salt and roll up the dough into a tight sausage.

Cut the sausage into 12 equal-sized slices and place them, cut-side up, into the prepared baking tin. Cover with clingfilm and set aside to prove in a warm place for 45 minutes to 1 hour, or until the rolls are touching each other and feel puffy to the touch.

Meanwhile, preheat the oven to 190°C (375°F), Gas Mark 5.

Bake the buns for 30–35 minutes, or until golden brown.

Meanwhile, make the syrup. Place the sugar and 60ml (¼ cup) water in a small saucepan and cook over a low heat just until the sugar has dissolved. Remove from the heat and add the vanilla.

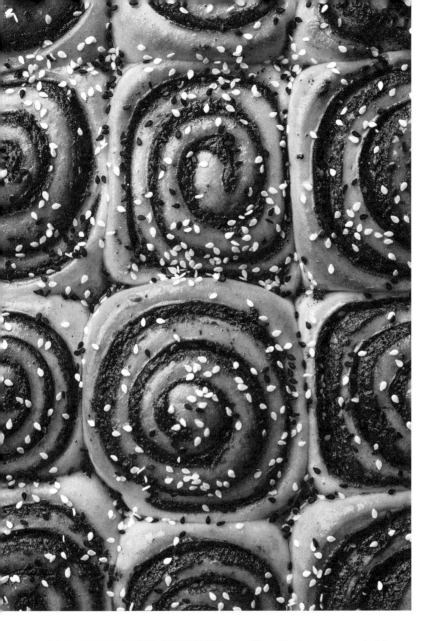

NOTE Make the dough a day before you want to bake the buns as it needs to chill in the refrigerator overnight.

When the buns come out of the oven, while still hot, liberally brush them with the syrup and then sprinkle over the sesame seeds. Leave the buns to cool completely in the tin before removing and serving.

Stored covered, these buns will keep for 2–3 days.

LAMINATED NECTARINE AND RASPBERRY BUCKWHEAT SCONES

MAKES 6

Don't let the word laminated put you off making this recipe. Lamination is the way a croissant dough is made, taking hours of effort and a high degree of skill, but this is a much simpler recipe that just uses that idea to add in the flavourings, namely nectarine and raspberry, in layers, creating a tender and flaky scone.

230g (8oz/1¾ cups + 1 tablespoon) plain (all-purpose) flour, plus extra for dusting

180g (6¼oz/1⅔ cups) buckwheat flour

1 tablespoon baking powder

50g (1¾oz/¼ cup) caster (superfine) sugar

½ teaspoon fine sea salt

140g (5oz/1¼ sticks) unsalted butter, chilled and diced

120ml (4fl oz/½ cup) sour cream

3 large eggs

2 teaspoons vanilla extract

120ml (4fl oz/½ cup) raspberry jam

3 nectarines (ripe but still a little firm), stoned and diced

demerara sugar, for sprinkling

Preheat the oven to 180°C (350°F), Gas Mark 4. Line the base of the baking tin with a piece of parchment paper.

To make the scone dough, mix together both flours, the baking powder, sugar and salt in a large bowl. Rub in the butter until it resembles coarse breadcrumbs, with a few larger flakes. Whisk the sour cream, two of the eggs and the vanilla together in a large jug, then drizzle this into the flour mixture, stirring with a round-bladed knife until the dough starts to clump together. Tip it out on to a lightly floured work surface and bring together to form a dough, then roll out into a 35 x 25cm (14 x 10in) rectangle with a short side facing you. Fold the top third of the dough down over the middle third and the bottom third up and over the other two thirds, like folding a business letter. Wrap in clingfilm and refrigerate for 20 minutes.

Roll out the dough on a lightly floured work surface into a 25cm (10in) square. Brush the left-hand side two-thirds of the dough with the jam and scatter over the diced nectarine, pressing it in a little to help it stick. Take the uncoated third of dough and fold it over to the centre, covering a portion of the jam/fruit-covered dough. Take the remaining left-hand side of the dough and fold that over, covering the other two portions, again like folding a business letter.

Gently use your rolling pin to flatten the dough just a little to seal everything together – the width of the folded dough shouldn't be more than 9–10cm (3½–4in). Cut it into three squares and then cut each square into two triangles. Transfer to the prepared tin. Lightly beat the remaining egg and brush over the top of each scone, then sprinkle liberally with demerara sugar.

Bake for 20–25 minutes, or until golden brown. Leave to cool slightly in the tin before serving warm.

These scones are best served on the day they are made, but they will keep in a sealed container for 2–3 days. Gently warm in the oven before serving.

ALMOST DOUGHNUTS

MAKES 9

Nothing quite compares to a freshly-fried, custard-filled doughnut, but these come pretty darn close! To get something similar to that light, airy texture of a fried doughnut, the logical choice was a brioche dough, infused with a little orange zest for added flavour. The filling is a classic pastry cream lightened with a little whipped cream, which gives it an ice-cream vibe.

FOR THE BRIOCHE DOUGH

375g (13¼oz/3 cups) plain (all-purpose) flour, plus extra for dusting

1 tablespoon caster (superfine) sugar

¾ teaspoon fine sea salt

1 teaspoon fast-action dried yeast

160ml (6fl oz/⅔ cups) whole milk

2 large eggs

finely grated zest of 1 orange

75g (2¾oz/5 tablespoons) unsalted butter, at room temperature, plus extra for greasing

FOR THE CUSTARD FILLING

180ml (6½fl oz/¾ cups) whole milk

3 large egg yolks

75g (2¾oz/6 tablespoons) caster (superfine) sugar

1½ tablespoons cornflour (cornstarch)

1 teaspoon vanilla bean paste

120ml (4fl oz/½ cup) double (heavy) cream

FOR THE CINNAMON SUGAR

45g (1½oz/3 tablespoons) unsalted butter

100g (3½oz/½ cup) caster (superfine) sugar

2 teaspoons ground cinnamon

To make the brioche dough, add the flour, sugar, salt and yeast to the bowl of an electric stand mixer with the dough hook attachment and mix briefly to combine. Add the milk, eggs and orange zest and knead on medium-low speed for about 10 minutes, or until the dough is smooth, elastic and pulling away from the sides of the bowl. With the mixer still running, add the butter, a little bit at a time. Once the butter has been worked into the dough, continue kneading for a further 10 minutes or so until the dough is once again pulling away from the sides of the bowl. Place the dough in a lightly greased bowl, cover with clingfilm and refrigerate overnight or for up to 2 days. If you prefer, you can let the dough rise at room temperature, but it's worth making this in advance as the dough is much easier to handle when thoroughly chilled.

Make the custard filling a day in advance, too. Pour the milk into a saucepan and bring to a simmer over a medium-high heat. Meanwhile, whisk together the remaining ingredients, except the cream, in a heatproof bowl for a couple of minutes until smooth and combined. Pour the hot milk over the egg mixture, whisking to prevent curdling. Return to the pan and cook, whisking constantly, until bubbling and thickened. Scrape the custard into a clean bowl, press a sheet of clingfilm onto the surface of the custard and refrigerate until needed.

To make the 'doughnuts', lightly grease and line the base of the baking tin with a piece of parchment paper. Divide the dough into nine equal-sized pieces (I weigh the dough so all the pieces are exactly the same size). Form each piece into a ball and place into the tin in three rows of three. Cover with clingfilm and set aside to prove in a warm place for an hour, or until the buns have almost doubled in size. To test if the dough has fully proved, press one of the buns with a lightly floured finger. The indentation should slowly spring back but not fully.

Meanwhile, preheat the oven to 190°C (375°F), Gas Mark 5.

Bake the buns for 15–18 minutes, or until golden brown. Meanwhile, melt the butter, and make the cinnamon sugar by mixing the sugar and cinnamon together in a small bowl.

NOTE Make the dough and custard a day before you want to make the 'doughnuts' as both need to chill in the refrigerator overnight.

Brush the buns liberally with the melted butter. Sprinkle the cinnamon sugar liberally over the top, then set aside to cool completely in the tin.

When you are ready to fill the 'doughnuts', finish the custard filling. Whip the cream in a bowl until it just holds soft peaks. Beat the custard to loosen, then fold in the whipped cream. Transfer to a piping bag fitted with a small round piping nozzle. Pierce the top of each 'doughnut' with a knife, insert the piping bag and fill with custard.

These are at their best when served close to making, but definitely on the same day.

STOLLEN-ISH BUNS

MAKES 12

I love the idea of stollen, the spiced sweet bread dough filled generously with marzipan, but more often than not I just can't get on board with how dense and heavy it is. To get past that, I use a fruit-rich brioche to make a lighter, more bread-like version.

The dough needs to chill overnight, so start this recipe the day before you want to bake it.

FOR THE STOLLEN-ISH DOUGH

1 batch of brioche dough (see page 152)

finely grated zest of 1 lemon

½ teaspoon ground cardamom

½ teaspoon ground cinnamon

⅛ teaspoon ground cloves

50g (1¾oz/½ cup) candied peel, chopped

175g (6oz/1⅓ cups) raisins

unsalted butter or neutral-tasting oil, for greasing

plain (all-purpose) flour, for dusting

1 egg, beaten with a splash of milk, for glazing

FOR THE FILLING AND TOPPING

185g (6½oz) marzipan

45g (1½oz/3 tablespoons) unsalted butter, melted

60g (2¼oz/½ cup) icing (powdered) sugar

Make the brioche according to the instructions on page 152, adding the lemon zest and ground spices with the other dry ingredients. When the butter has been added and the dough kneaded for the final time, add the candied peel and raisins and knead briefly until evenly distributed. Place the dough into a lightly greased bowl, cover with clingfilm and refrigerate overnight, or for at least 8 hours.

In the morning, lightly grease the baking tin and line the base with a piece of parchment paper.

Divide the marzipan into 12 equal-sized pieces and roll into balls. Turn the chilled dough out on to a lightly floured work surface, then press into a flat square. Cut the dough into 12 equal-sized pieces and roll into balls, then cover with clingfilm to prevent them from drying out. Working with one piece of dough at a time, flatten it into a disc. Add a ball of marzipan to the middle, then fold the sides of the dough up and over the marzipan, pinch the edges together to seal and re-shape into a ball.

Place the filled balls of dough into the prepared tin, leaving a little space between each one. Cover the tin with clingfilm and set aside in a warm place for 1–2 hours, until the dough has almost doubled in size (all the fruit in the dough can slow down the rise).

Preheat the oven to 190°C (375°F), Gas Mark 5.

Brush the risen buns with the egg and milk glaze. Bake for 15–20 minutes until the buns are golden brown.

Immediately brush the buns with the melted butter, then dust generously with the icing sugar. Leave to cool slightly in the tin, then remove and serve warm or cold.

Store in a sealed container for 3–4 days.

APPLE FRITTER MONKEY BREAD

SERVES 10–12

Monkey bread is a cousin to doughnuts and a brother to cinnamon buns but exists as its own special thing. So named because it's supposedly finger food, meaning even monkeys could eat it, it's definitely a great dish for a special brunch. My favourite way to make this is to prep the dough the night before and rest it in the refrigerator overnight, meaning with a short amount of work the following morning, you have a warm, toasty smell filling the house as people wake up.

The brioche dough ideally needs to chill overnight, so start this recipe the day before you want to bake it.

FOR THE BRIOCHE DOUGH

500g (1lb 2oz/4 cups) plain (all-purpose) flour

50g (1¾oz/¼ cup) caster (superfine) sugar

2 teaspoons fine sea salt

7g (¼oz/2¼ teaspoons) fast-action dried yeast

165ml (5¾fl oz/⅔ cup + 1 teaspoon) whole milk

3 large eggs

85g (3oz/¾ stick) unsalted butter, at room temperature, diced

FOR THE COATING

125g (4½oz/9 tablespoons) unsalted butter, melted

220g (8oz/1 cup) light brown sugar

1 tablespoon ground cinnamon

FOR THE CARAMELIZED APPLES

3 Granny Smith apples (roughly 375g/13¼oz/3 cups), peeled, cored and diced

45g (1½oz/3 tablespoons) unsalted butter

50g (1¾oz/¼ cups) light brown sugar

For the brioche dough, place the flour, sugar, salt and yeast into the bowl of an electric stand mixer with the dough hook attachment and mix briefly to combine. Pour in the milk and eggs and mix together to form a shaggy dough, then on low-medium speed, knead for 10–15 minutes until smooth and elastic. With the mixer running slowly, add in the butter, a piece or two at a time, working it into the dough, then knead for a further 10–15 minutes until smooth and elastic.

Tip the dough into a large, clean bowl, cover with clingfilm and refrigerate overnight (at least 8 hours) or for up to 2 days. If you prefer, you can let the dough rise at room temperature, but it's worth making this in advance as the dough is much easier to handle when thoroughly chilled.

To make the caramelized apples, melt the butter in a small saucepan with the sugar. Once melted, add the apples and cook for 5–8 minutes, until softened. Scrape into a bowl, cover and refrigerate until needed.

Press or roll the chilled dough into a disc about 1cm (½in) thick.

For the coating, place the melted butter into a small bowl, then mix the sugar and cinnamon together in a separate bowl.

Cut the dough into 2.5cm (1in) squares. Roll each piece into a ball then, working with a couple of dough balls at a time, dip them first into the melted butter and then into the cinnamon sugar to fully coat, then place in the baking tin, adding spoonfuls of apple as you go. Once all the buns and apples have been added, you can drizzle over any remaining butter and cinnamon sugar. Cover the tin with clingfilm and set aside in a warm place for about 1 hour, or until doubled in size.

CONTINUED OVERLEAF

FOR THE GLAZE

100g (3½oz/¾ cup) icing (powdered) sugar

½ teaspoon vanilla bean paste

Preheat the oven to 190°C (375°F), Gas Mark 5.

Bake the monkey bread for 20–25 minutes, or until golden. Leave to cool slightly in the tin before glazing.

For the glaze, mix the icing sugar and vanilla with a little cold water, adding enough water until the glaze is the consistency of honey. Drizzle the glaze liberally over the monkey bread and serve while it's still a little warm.

This bread is best served on the day it's made.

STRAWBERRY SHORTCAKES

SERVES 8

Shortcakes or buttermilk biscuits, split and served with strawberries and cream, are one of my top summertime desserts. They celebrate strawberries when they're at their best and they're incredibly easy to make. Now to confuse things a little, biscuits in the US are closer to UK scones, then US scones are similar to their UK cousins, so you can almost think of this as a US version of a cream tea.

FOR THE SHORTCAKES (BUTTERMILK BISCUITS)

350g (12oz/1¾ cups + 1 tablespoon) self-raising flour, plus extra for dusting

2 tablespoons caster (superfine) sugar

½ teaspoon bicarbonate of soda (baking soda)

½ teaspoon fine sea salt

125g (4½oz/9 tablespoons) unsalted butter, diced and chilled

300ml (10fl oz/1½ cups) buttermilk, plus a little extra for the glaze

demerara sugar, for sprinkling

TO SERVE

285g (10oz) fresh strawberries

2 tablespoons caster (superfine) sugar

300ml (10fl oz/1¼ cups) double (heavy) cream

2 teaspoons vanilla bean paste

NOTE If you want to freeze the shortcakes, make them up to where you cut them into squares, then place on a baking tray lined with parchment paper and freeze until solid before transferring to a freezer bag. They'll keep for up to a month. You can then bake them straight from the freezer (as above), adding an extra 5 minutes or so to the baking time.

Before starting the shortcakes, slice the strawberries and toss together in a bowl with the sugar, then set aside to macerate. This makes a healthy amount of filling, but a strawberry shortcake should be overflowing with fruit as far as I'm concerned.

For the shortcakes, place the flour, sugar, bicarbonate of soda and salt into a large bowl and whisk together to combine. Add the butter and toss to coat, then use your hands to press the butter into flat pieces, rubbing it in a little so that the flour is coated in fat. Refrigerate for 15 minutes.

Remove from the refrigerator and drizzle in the buttermilk, a little at a time, stirring together with a round-bladed knife until the mixture is starting to hold together. Tip it out on to a lightly floured work surface and gently bring together to form a dough. Roll out into a 20 x 50cm (8 x 20in) rectangle, then fold in thirds, like a business letter. Turn the dough through 90 degrees and repeat the rolling and folding a second time. Wrap the dough in clingfilm and freeze for 20 minutes.

Preheat the oven to 220°C (425°F), Gas Mark 9. Line the base of the baking tin with a piece of parchment paper.

Place the chilled dough on to a lightly floured work surface, then roll out into a rectangle about 2.5cm (1in) thick. Cut into eight squares and place into the prepared tin, in two rows of four. Brush the tops with a little extra buttermilk and sprinkle liberally with demerara sugar.

Bake for 15–20 minutes, or until golden brown. Transfer the shortcakes to a wire rack to cool.

To serve, lightly whip the cream and vanilla together in a bowl, just until holding soft peaks. Split the shortcakes in half and sandwich with a dollop of whipped cream and the macerated strawberries.

These shortcakes are best served on the day they're made, soon after assembling.

CRÈME FRAÎCHE BRIOCHE FRUIT TART

SERVES 8–10

This dish is inspired by a Nancy Silverton recipe that was so beloved by Julia Child that it made her cry when it was made on her 90s TV show *Baking with Julia*. Upon tasting, Child shed a tear and declared it the best dessert she had ever tried. High praise indeed. My version, a brioche tart topped with a crème fraîche custard and a scattering of fruit, is in the same spirit as the original but simplified slightly, baking the fruit right on the custard layer.

The brioche dough needs to chill overnight, so start this recipe the day before you want to bake it.

FOR THE BRIOCHE DOUGH

265g (9½oz/2⅛ cups) plain (all-purpose) flour, plus extra for dusting

25g (1oz/⅛ cup) caster (superfine) sugar

¾ teaspoon fine sea salt

5g (⅛oz/1½ teaspoons) fast-action dried yeast

60ml (2¼fl oz/¼ cup) whole milk

2 large eggs

100g (3½fl oz/7 tablespoons) unsalted butter, at room temperature, diced, plus extra for greasing

FOR THE TOPPING

180ml (6¼fl oz/¾ cup) crème fraîche

1 large egg

65g (2½oz/⅓ cup) caster (superfine) sugar

1 teaspoon vanilla bean paste

2 nectarines, halved, stones removed and cut into slices

300g (10½oz) mixed fresh blackberries and raspberries

1 large egg yolk, beaten, for glazing

pearl sugar, for sprinkling (see Note)

NOTE If you can't find pearl sugar (or sugar nibs), you can use sanding sugar, demerara sugar or even flaked almonds.

For the brioche dough, place the flour, sugar, salt and yeast into the bowl of an electric stand mixer with the dough hook attachment and mix briefly to combine. Pour in the milk and eggs and mix together to form a shaggy dough, then on low-medium speed, knead for 10–15 minutes until smooth and elastic. With the mixer still running, add the butter, a piece or two at a time, working it into the dough, then knead for a further 10–15 minutes until smooth and elastic and pulling away from the sides of the bowl.

To make life simpler, we're going to refrigerate the dough overnight to make it easier to handle and roll out. Tip the dough into a large, lightly greased bowl, cover with clingfilm and refrigerate overnight (at least 8 hours) or for up to 2 days.

Lightly grease the baking tin and line the base with a piece of parchment paper.

When you are ready to make the tart, roll out the chilled dough on a lightly floured work surface into a 25 x 35cm (10 x 14in) rectangle. Gently drape the dough into the prepared baking tin with the excess going up the sides, almost like you are lining a tart tin with pastry. Cover with clingfilm and set aside in a warm place for about 1 hour, or until almost doubled in size.

Preheat the oven to 190°C (375°F), Gas Mark 5.

For the topping, whisk together the crème fraîche, egg, sugar and vanilla in a measuring jug until smooth. Uncover the brioche and use your fingertips to dimple the centre of the dough, like you're making focaccia. Pour in the custard mixture, then scatter over the fruit. Brush the brioche border with the beaten egg yolk and sprinkle with pearl sugar.

Bake for 20–25 minutes, or until the custard is set around the edges and just a little wobbly in the middle and the brioche border is golden.

Leave the tart to cool completely in the tin, then cut into portions and serve. Store covered for 1–2 days.

RASPBERRY AND ROSE CHEESECAKE BUNS

MAKES 12

Raspberry and rose is, to me, one of the classic flavour combinations. Rose can seem old-fashioned, even soapy, but when done right, with restraint, I think it adds a little magic and sophistication to raspberries. It also reminds me of my favourite croissants in Paris, made with this combination of flavours by the incredible pastry chef Pierre Hermé.

The brioche dough ideally needs to chill overnight, so start this recipe the day before you want to bake it.

FOR THE BRIOCHE DOUGH

500g (1lb 2oz/4 cups) strong white bread flour, plus extra for dusting

25g (1oz/⅛ cup) caster (superfine) sugar

1 teaspoon fine sea salt

7g (¼oz/2¼ teaspoons) fast-action dried yeast

250ml (9fl oz/1 cup + 2 teaspoons) whole milk

2 large eggs

100g (3½oz/7 tablespoons) unsalted butter, at room temperature, diced

FOR THE FILLING

30g (1oz/2 tablespoons) unsalted butter, very soft

150g (5½oz/⅔ cup) full-fat cream cheese, at room temperature

240g (8¾oz/¾ cup) raspberry jam

For the brioche dough, place the flour, sugar, salt and yeast into the bowl of an electric stand mixer with the dough hook attachment and mix briefly to combine. Pour in the milk and eggs and mix together to form a shaggy dough, then on low-medium speed, knead for 10–15 minutes until smooth and elastic. With the mixer running slowly, add in the butter, a piece or two at a time, working it into the dough, then knead for a further 10–15 minutes until smooth and elastic and pulling away from the sides of the bowl.

Tip the dough into a large, lightly greased bowl, cover with clingfilm and refrigerate overnight (for at least 8 hours) or for up to 2 days. If you prefer, you can let the dough rise at room temperature, but it's worth making this in advance as the dough is much easier to handle when thoroughly chilled.

Line the base of the baking tin with parchment paper.

Roll out the chilled dough on a lightly floured work surface into a 40 x 50cm (16 x 20in) rectangle. Beat together the butter and cream cheese for the filling and spread over the dough, then spread the jam evenly over the top. Tightly roll up the dough (starting from a long edge) into a long sausage, then cut into 12 equal-sized slices (using unflavoured dental floss will make the cleanest cuts) and place, cut-side up, in the prepared tin. Cover with clingfilm and leave to prove in a warm place for 45 minutes–1 hour or until the rolls are touching each other and feel puffy to the touch.

Preheat the oven to 190°C (375°F), Gas Mark 5.

Bake the buns for 30–35 minutes, or until golden brown. Set aside while you make the glaze.

CONTINUED OVERLEAF

FOR THE GLAZE AND DECORATION

30g (1oz/2 tablespoons) unsalted butter

2 tablespoons lemon juice

1 teaspoon vanilla bean paste

pinch of fine sea salt

225g (8oz/1¾ cups + 2 tablespoons) icing (powdered) sugar

2 teaspoons rose water

2 tablespoons edible dried rose petals

2 tablespoons chopped (shelled) pistachios

Place the butter, lemon juice, vanilla and salt in a small saucepan over a medium heat and stir together until everything has melted and just starts to bubble. Remove from the heat and stir in the icing sugar and rose water until smooth.

While the buns are still warm, brush the glaze all over them. Finish with a sprinkling of rose petals and chopped pistachios. Remove from the tin and serve warm or cold.

Store in a sealed container for 2–3 days.

SLAB SCONE

SERVES 8–10

British folk can't agree on how to correctly pronounce the word scone or even whether the jam or cream should go on first, so this slab scone will be sacrilege for some, but I love it, as it turns a dainty afternoon tea staple into a perfect summertime dessert. Of course, I have kept the clotted cream, it is after all one of the best tasting things in the world. For the topping, however, I have lightened it up a tad using fresh macerated strawberries with a little hint of vanilla instead of the more traditional jam.

If you can't get clotted cream you can also use mascarpone or whipped cream, but just do me one favour, if there is clotted cream available that is made in Devon and you're not in the UK, then don't buy it, it will have been sterilized and pasteurized and the flavour is a shadow of the real deal and not worth the disappointment.

FOR THE SLAB SCONE

500g (1lb 2oz/4 cups) self-raising flour, plus extra for dusting

1½ teaspoons baking powder

50g (1¾oz/¼ cup) caster (superfine) sugar

½ teaspoon fine sea salt

finely grated zest of 1 large lemon

150g (5½oz/1⅓ sticks) unsalted butter, chilled and diced

120ml (4fl oz/½ cup) whole milk, plus a splash for the egg wash

3 large eggs, beaten + 1 large egg

2 tablespoons demerara sugar

FOR THE TOPPING

400g (14oz) fresh strawberries, hulled and halved

25g (1oz/⅛ cup) caster (superfine) sugar

½ teaspoon vanilla bean paste

340g (11¾oz) clotted cream

Preheat the oven to 190°C (375°F), Gas Mark 5. Line the base of the baking tin with a strip of parchment paper that overhangs the two long sides of the tin, securing in place with metal clips.

For the slab scone, mix the flour, baking powder, sugar, salt and lemon zest together in a large bowl, then rub in the butter until it resembles coarse breadcrumbs with a few larger pieces remaining. Make a well in the middle and pour in the milk and the beaten egg mixture, stirring to form a soft but not sticky dough.

Tip the dough out on to a lightly floured work surface, press or roll into a 23 x 33cm (9 x 13in) rectangle and transfer to the prepared tin. Beat the remaining egg with a splash of milk to form an egg wash, and brush over the top of the scone, then sprinkle liberally with the demerara sugar.

Bake for 20–25 minutes, or until golden brown. Set aside to cool completely in the tin.

Meanwhile, prepare the topping. Place the strawberries into a large bowl and sprinkle over the sugar and vanilla, stirring together briefly. Leave to macerate for 30 minutes–1 hour, until the sugar has dissolved.

Once cool, remove the scone from the tin, spread the clotted cream all over the scone and then top with the macerated strawberries, drizzling with the syrup that is left in the bottom of the bowl. Cut into portions and serve.

This slab scone is best served on the day it's made, soon after assembling.

MATCHA PAN

MAKES 12

Inspired by one of my top Japanese snacks, the curry pan (effectively curry-filled doughnuts), these are a baked sweet version, filled with a matcha white chocolate ganache instead of the usual curry. The bread is a Japanese milk bread made using the tangzhong method, a simple way to make a super soft and longer-lasting bread dough. The curry pan are usually coated in panko breadcrumbs and fried. I go so far as coating in the breadcrumbs, but these are baked instead of fried.

FOR THE GANACHE FILLING

300g (10½oz) white chocolate, finely chopped

180ml (6¼fl oz/¾ cup) double (heavy) cream

2 teaspoons matcha powder

FOR THE JAPANESE MILK BREAD

375g (13oz/3 cups) strong white bread flour, plus extra for dusting

240ml (8½fl oz/1 cup) whole milk

1 teaspoon fine sea salt

3 tablespoons milk powder

7g (¼oz/2¼ teaspoons) fast-action dried yeast

3 tablespoons caster (superfine) sugar

2 large eggs

60g (2¼oz/4½ tablespoons) unsalted butter, at room temperature, plus extra for greasing

6 tablespoons panko breadcrumbs

Before making the bread, you need to make the ganache as it needs time to set. Place the chocolate in a heatproof bowl and set aside. Add the cream to a small saucepan and bring to a simmer. Add the matcha to a small, heatproof bowl, pour over a little of the hot cream and whisk to a smooth paste. Scrape this back into the pan and whisk until combined. Pour the hot matcha cream over the chocolate and set aside for a couple of minutes, then stir together to form a smooth, silky ganache. Refrigerate while you make the dough.

For the milk bread, add 4 tablespoons of the flour and about 80ml (3fl oz/⅓ cup) of the milk to a small saucepan. Mix constantly over a medium heat until it forms a thick, gluey paste, then scrape it into a small, heatproof bowl and leave to cool slightly.

Place the remaining flour, the salt, milk powder, yeast and sugar into the bowl of an electric stand mixer with the dough hook attachment and mix briefly to combine. Add the remaining milk, one egg and the flour paste and knead together on low-medium speed for about 10 minutes to form a smooth, elastic dough. Mix in the butter, then knead for a further 10 minutes until the dough is elastic and no longer sticking to the bowl. Tip the dough into a lightly greased large bowl, cover with clingfilm and set aside in a warm place for about 1 hour, or until doubled in size.

Line the base of the baking tin with a piece of parchment paper.

Tip the dough out on to a lightly floured work surface and knock back, then divide into 12 equal pieces. Roll each piece of dough into a ball, then cover with clingfilm to prevent them from drying out.

Working with one piece of dough at a time, flatten it into a disc. Add a little dollop of the chilled ganache to the middle, then fold the sides of the dough over the ganache, pinch the edges together to seal and re-shape into a ball.

CONTINUED OVERLEAF

Place the filled balls of dough into the prepared tin in four rows of three. Cover with clingfilm and set aside in a warm place for 1–1½ hours, or until the buns have almost doubled in size (the ganache will be cold so the dough will take a little extra time to rise).

Preheat the oven to 190°C (375°F), Gas Mark 5.

Brush the buns with the remaining beaten egg and sprinkle liberally with the panko breadcrumbs. Bake for 18–20 minutes, or until golden brown. Leave to cool in the tin before serving.

Store in a sealed container for 2–3 days.

FLORENTINE GRAPE FOCACCIA

SERVES 8–10

I have a habit of spending my time abroad making endless lists of recipe ideas from the things I've seen, eaten and want to eat. This focaccia, based on Schiacciata all'uva from Florence, is a very seasonal and very special recipe. Seasonal because the grapes traditionally used, fragolina, are only available for a particularly short window. Special because they have a candy-like flavour, so much so they go by the name 'strawberry grapes'. My version is not traditional as I add rosemary and demerara sugar, but the spirit of this recipe definitely resides in Florence. If you can't find fragolina grapes, then any dark grapes will work, but if you do find them, you know exactly what to make.

FOR THE FOCACCIA DOUGH

500g (1lb 2oz/4 cups) strong white bread flour

7g (¼oz/2¼ teaspoons) fast-action dried yeast

2 teaspoons fine sea salt

400ml (14floz/1⅔ cups) lukewarm water

4 teaspoons extra virgin olive oil, plus 2 tablespoons for greasing the tin

FOR THE GRAPE TOPPING

280g (10oz/2 cups) fragolina or any other dark grapes

1 sprig of rosemary, leaves picked and roughly chopped

4 tablespoons demerara sugar

2 tablespoons extra virgin olive oil

FOR THE MASCARPONE TOPPING (OPTIONAL)

115g (4oz/½ cup) mascarpone

1 teaspoon vanilla bean paste

1 tablespoon caster (superfine) sugar

For the focaccia dough, place the flour, yeast and salt into the bowl of an electric stand mixer with the dough hook attachment and mix briefly to combine. Pour in the warm water and 4 teaspoons of olive oil and mix together to form a shaggy dough, then on medium speed, knead for 10–15 minutes until smooth and elastic. Scrape the dough into a lightly greased bowl, cover with clingfilm and set aside in a warm place for about an hour, or until doubled in size.

Pour the 2 tablespoons of olive oil into the baking tin and use your fingers to rub it all over the base and up the sides. Tip the dough into the tin and use your fingertips to stretch and press it into an even layer. If the dough springs back and won't hold its shape, leave it to rest for a couple of minutes before continuing. Cover the tin and set aside to prove in a warm place for 45 minutes–1 hour, or until almost doubled in size.

Preheat the oven to 220°C (425°F), Gas Mark 7.

Using a wet hand, dimple the dough with your fingertips, scatter over the grapes, rosemary and sugar, then drizzle over the olive oil. If using the mascarpone topping, mix together the mascarpone, vanilla and sugar, then dollop this randomly over the bread.

Bake for 20–25 minutes, or until golden. Leave to cool completely in the tin before cutting into portions to serve.

This focaccia is best served on the day it's made, but will keep in a sealed container for a couple of days.

NOTE Traditionally it's common to leave the seeds in fragolina grapes, as they are very delicate and it's a bit tricky and time-consuming to remove the seeds. If you prefer to deseed them, then halve them and remove the seeds before use.

RESOURCES

THE TIN

Divertimenti
www.divertimenti.co.uk

Nordicware
www.nordicware.com
www.nordicware.com.au

GENERAL BAKEWARE

Divertimeti
www.divertimenti.co.uk

John Lewis
www.johnlewis.com

Williams Sonoma
www.williams-sonoma.com
www.williams-sonoma.com.au

Sur Le Table
www.surlatable.com

Kitchen Warehouse
www.kitchenwarehouse.com.au

BAKING STEELS

Pizza Steel
www.pizzasteel.com

Baking Steel Co
www.bakingsteel.com

Roc Baking Steel
www.rocbakingsteel.com.au

PISTACHIO/HAZELNUT PASTE

Nut Kitchen
www.thenutkitchen.com

King Arthur Flour
www.kingarthurflour.com

TAHINI

Belazu
www.belazu.co.uk

Seed and Mill
www.seedandmill.com

PEARL SUGAR

Sous Chef
www.souschef.co.uk

King Arthur Flour
www.kingarthurflour.com

ANCIENT GRAIN FLOURS (RYE, BUCKWHEAT ETC)

Doves Farm
www.dovesfarm.co.uk

King Arthur Flour
www.kingsrthurflour.com

Flour Leaf Milling
www.flourleafmilling.com.au

VANILLA PODS

Heilala Vanilla
www.heilalavanilla.com
www.amazon.co.uk

PASSION FRUIT PURÉE

Sous Chef
www.souschef.co.uk

Amazon
www.amazon.com

MATCHA POWDER

Japan Centre
www.japancentre.com

Aiya Matcha
www.aiyamatca.com

INGREDIENTS

BUTTER	I use butter that has at least 82% butterfat content and for every recipe in this book that means unsalted butter. I prefer unsalted butter as it means I can control the salt level of a recipe and because every brand of salted butter varies in its amount of salt.
SALT	I use two types of salt, fine sea salt and flaked sea salt. I avoid regular table salt as the flavour is poor, with acrid flavours. I generally use fine sea salt when it is going in a recipe and I want it to evenly flavour the entire bake. Flaked sea salt is great for sprinkling on top of recipes where a pop of salt helps to enhance the flavour. If you prefer not to sprinkle salt over a finished dish, as I sometimes do, you can of course omit this.
SUGAR	In this book I call for caster (superfine) sugar, a fine-grained white sugar. There are many names and styles for the different sized grains of sugar depending on where you are in the world and as a guide use the finest grain available for these recipes. Another sugar used is light brown sugar, which has the most wonderful, caramel-like flavour. When looking for brown sugars I prefer versions that are 'unrefined' (meaning they aren't white sugar with added molasses, but a sugar that hasn't had its natural molasses removed during processing) as the flavour tends to have more of that caramel, molasses-rich flavour. In the recipes I call for light brown sugar but you can happily switch this to light brown muscovado to get those richer flavours. The other sugar called for is icing sugar, which sometimes also goes by 10x or powdered sugar.

FLOUR

Most recipes use UK plain (all-purpose) flour which is a wheat flour with 8–10% protein. I occasionally use 'self-raising' flour, which is plain (all-purpose) flour with the addition of baking powder for leavening. If you're not in the UK and using a local version of self-raising flour, check the ingredients to see if it includes salt, which is often the case around the world. If so, reduce the salt in the recipe a little to compensate. If you can't find self-raising flour, you can make your own by adding 1½ teaspoons of baking powder to every 125g (1 cup) of plain (all-purpose) flour.

CHOCOLATE AND COCOA

All the recipes in this book use Dutch process cocoa powder. For those in Europe this is the standard style of cocoa powder, and what you generally find on supermarket shelves, but if you are presented with a choice between 'natural' and 'dutched', the flavour and colour of dutched is deeper and richer. If the label doesn't distinguish between the two styles, look for something that refers to alkalization (this might be listed as an ingredient or a process). You can also generally tell by the colour – natural cocoa powder has a dry, almost grey, powdery look and dutched cocoa tends to be a much deeper brown, sometimes as dark as black in colour. (The very darkest cocoa powder is known as black cocoa and is much harder to find, but can be used in these recipes if you prefer.)

When recipes specify a chocolate with a certain cocoa solid percentage that is because it has an effect on the overall taste and texture of a recipe. I don't give a specific percentage but a range which I prefer. If the chocolate is an addition, like in my Tahini Chocolate Chip Cookie Bars (see page 53), I generally recommend the type of chocolate rather than the percentage as the flavour is down to personal taste.

CREAM	I mainly use double cream, a whippable cream that has a 48% fat content. In the US/Canada the closest equivalent would be heavy cream or whipping cream and in Australia it would be also be double cream.
EGGS	All the eggs in these recipes are UK size large unless otherwise stated. This means they weigh roughly between 63–73g, which is the same in Europe. Outside of europe, including the US, Canada and Sustralia, this would generally mean using extra-large eggs
VANILLA	Vanilla is as key to a baker as pepper is to a cook, but over the last few years the price has shot through the roof. You will find I therefore call mainly for vanilla extract and bean paste, as these are more affordable.
GELATIN	There are not many recipes where gelatin is called for, but where gelatin is used, I find sheet gelatin easier to use and has less of an aftertaste. If you live where powdered is the dominant style of gelatin, you can substitute 3½ sheets for 1 tablespoon (1 envelope) of powdered gelatin.
YEAST	All recipes that call for yeast require fast-action dried yeast. This is a granulated style that comes in 7g/2½ teaspoons packets. Unlike active dry yeast, this does not need to be bloomed in water, it can be added straight to the dried ingredients. If you've had yeast at the back of your cupboard and can't remember the last time you used it, perhaps buy some more as over time yeast will lose its effectiveness.

EQUIPMENT

THE TIN

I am so happy that this section is just one paragraph long. Most baking books call for a lot of different tins or pans and for this book it's just one, a 23 x 33cm (9 x 13in) tin. This is a classic brownie tin and a lot of you may already have one in your kitchen. Every manufacturer is a little different and measures that size a little differently. As long as the tin is 5cm (2in) deep the recipes in this book will work wonderfully. My preference of material is aluminium and I prefer uncoated. I'm not a big fan of non-stick versions and I particularly avoid dark/black non-stick coatings (they tend to be poor-quality, the black colour often over-browns recipes and they bake quicker than recipes call for).

STAND MIXER

I use an electric stand mixer in these recipes. I love these machines as they make baking quicker and easier, but an electric hand mixer will also do a wonderful job, you'll just need to extend the time called for mixing a little as they tend to be less efficient. The only recipes I don't advise using a hand mixer for are the brioche-style bakes as most hand mixers struggle with enriched doughs. For these recipes I prefer kneading by hand if I don't have a stand mixer.

BAKING STONE/ STEEL

I like to bake all the pastry recipes atop either a baking stone or baking steel that has been preheated in the oven, which will help ensure the pastry base is never soggy. If you don't have either of these a baking tray will also help.

OVEN THERMOMETER

All temperatures listed are for a standard oven, if using a convention oven you may want to reduce the temperature by 20 degrees (if using celsius) as these ovens are more efficient than regular ovens. As most ovens tend to run either a little hot or a little cold, despite what the dial suggests, investing in an oven thermometer will help you know how hot your oven actually runs.

INDEX

ABOUT THE AUTHOR

Edd Kimber is a baker and food writer based in London. He is the author of *The Boy Who Bakes* (2011), *Say It With Cake* (2012), and *Patisserie Made Simple* (2014). Over the last ten years he has appeared on multiple television shows including as resident baker on *The Alan Titchmarsh Show*, on *Sunday Brunch*, *Perfect* and on the original series of *The Great British Bake Off* of which he is the inaugural winner. He regularly shares his knowledge at cookery schools and at food festivals around the world and also writes for multiple publications. Edd is the go-to baking writer for *Olive* Magazine and a contributer to *Bake From Scratch* magazine.

@THEBOYWHOBAKES
WWW.THEBOYWHOBAKES.CO.UK

ACKNOWLEDGEMENTS

Firstly, I have to express the largest amount of thanks to everyone who reads my books, everyone who is excited when I post a new recipe on my website and rushes to the kitchen to make it. The book would quite literally not exist without you and your enthusiasm for my recipes. My one goal with my baking has always been to encourage others to get in the kitchen and bake, to share in the enjoyment it can bring, to be that helping hand helping you gain the confidence to say 'I can make this'. I hope this book is filled with recipes you'll use for years to come.

Mike, even though you have an irrational dislike of cardamom and cinnamon which deeply concerns me, you have been my biggest cheerleader, a level-headed voice when I need reassurance, or when the workload has felt like a mountain I'm struggling to climb. You have tried just about everything in this book and have always given me the honest feedback I need. I would have gone stir-crazy doing this alone, so thank you for always being there, and especially for putting up with a messy house this year. I love you very much.

To the friends, colleagues and even strangers that I've foisted cakes and cookies upon, thank you for being my guinea pigs even if it's difficult to enjoy when I'm staring at you waiting for a reaction and a full breakdown of your opinion. Writing a cookbook can be a strangely solitary project and seeing people enjoying the recipes really reminds me why I love this job. To Clare Ptak, Dan Lepard, Joy Wilson and Helen Goh, thank you for believing in the book and lending your voice, I am forever grateful. Nik Sharma, thanks for being that voice across the Atlantic who understood the work that goes into writing a book and commiserating with me when the stress was a bit much.

Simon, you're one of the people I will always trust to be honest with your opinion and I know I can always ask you for your thoughts and opinions and bounce ideas off you, thank you.

My agent Katherine Stonehouse, it's been a long road and you've never stopped pushing. I appreciate all your hard work in getting this project off the ground and always believing in me, I can't thank you enough.

To Evi, thank you so much for casting your design magic over the book, I love the finished product and cannot wait to see it out in the world. To everyone at Kyle Books, especially Isabel and Judith, thanks for letting me loose on a fourth book and and giving me the freedom to take the idea and run with it. I think we have produced something special and I'm especially proud that you let me stretch my creativity and not only write the book but photograph it as well.